THE STATUS OF MORALITY

THOMAS L. CARSON

Department of Philosophy,
Virginia Polytechnic Institute and State University

THE STATUS OF
MORALITY

D. REIDEL PUBLISHING COMPANY

A MEMBER OF THE KLUWER ACADEMIC PUBLISHERS GROUP

DORDRECHT / BOSTON / LANCASTER

231955

Library of Congress Cataloging in Publication Data **CIP**

Carson, Thomas L., 1950–
    The status of morality.

    (Philosophical studies series in philosophy; v. 31)
    Bibliography: p.
    Includes index.
    1. Ethics. I. Title. II. Series.
    BJ1012.C33   1984   170'.42   84–4717
    ISBN 90–277–1691–9

Published by D. Reidel Publishing Company,
P.O. Box 17, 3300 AA Dordrecht, Holland.

Sold and distributed in the U.S.A. and Canada
by Kluwer Academic Publishers,
190 Old Derby Street, Hingham, MA 02043, U.S.A.

In all other countries, sold and distributed
by Kluwer Academic Publishers Group,
P.O. Box 322, 3300 AH Dordrecht, Holland.

Printed in The Netherlands.

For Judy

TABLE OF CONTENTS

PREFACE

My interest in the issues considered here arose out of my great frustration in trying to attack the all-pervasive relativism of my students in introductory ethics courses at Virginia Polytechnic Institute and State University. I am grateful to my students for forcing me to take moral relativism and skepticism seriously and for compelling me to argue for my own dogmatically maintained version of moral objectivism. The result is before the reader. The conclusions reached here (which can be described either as a minimal objectivism or as a moderate verson of relativism) are considerably weaker than those that I had expected and would have liked to have defended. I have arrived at these views kicking and screaming and have resisted them to the best of my ability. The arguments of this book are directed at those who deny that moral judgments can ever be correct (in any sense that is opposed to mistaken) and who also deny that we are ever rationally compelled to accept one moral judgment as opposed to another. I have sought to take their views seriously and to fight them on their own grounds without making use of any assumptions that they would be unwilling to grant. My conclusion is that, while it is possible to refute the kind of extreme irrationalism that one often encounters, it is impossible to defend the kind of objectivist meta-ethical views that most of us want to hold, without begging the question against the non-objectivist.

My work on this book has been supported by a fellowship from the National Endowment for the Humanities from July 1980– July 1981. The greater portion of the manuscript was completed during that time. I have profited greatly from the advice and criticism of numerous friends and colleagues. I am pleased to acknowledge these debts here. I am indebted to Mark Overvold and Mitchell Silver for many helpful discussions of the topics considered in the book and for many helpful criticisms of Chapters One, Two, and Three. I am also greatly indebted to Roderick Firth for a careful reading and penetrating criticisms of Chapter Two. It is his work and that of Brentano and Richard Brandt that has most influenced my own. Roderick Chisholm read Chapter One and helped me with my interpretation of Brentano. Harlan Miller's careful reading of the entire manuscript has saved me from many errors of both style and substance. Marcia Baron also offered most helpful criticisms of Chapter One and my interpretation of Nietzsche. My colleagues Bill Williams, Eleonore Stump, and Norman Grover have read numerous drafts of the Chapter Three which has benefited from their criticisms as well as those of B.C. Postow. John Wilcox offered helpful advice on several important matters relating to Nietzsche. Anne Kierstead offered helpful advice on many questions of style. I also wish to thank Dan Brock, Judy Covey, Noah Lemos, and John Wander for many helpful discussions and difficult questions concerning my version of the ideal observer theory. Less direct, but no less significant are my debts to my teachers at Saint Olaf College and Brown University. I wish to thank Dean Robert Paterson and Virginia Polytechnic Institute and State University for securing me the first rate typing services of Rebecca Cox. I am also grateful to Harlan Miller (again) for his most generous assistance with the word-processing system at VPI & SU.

Finally, I wish to acknowledge my special indebtedness to my parents and family whose unwavering love and encouragement have always sustained me. I dedicate this book to Judy with love.

INTRODUCTION

This book is concerned with questions about the status of moral judgments. Here, I will indicate the kinds of questions that I will be concerned with and then outline the answers that the book attempts to provide.

Disagreement about moral questions is a major impetus to reflection about the status of morality. When one finds other people who hold views about moral questions that conflict with one's own, then one is compelled to ask whether one's own views are correct, whether this implies that the views of those with whom one disagrees are incorrect, and if so, how one knows this. The apparent unresolvability of disagreements about moral questions has led many people to become moral relativists. According to the moral relativist (or meta-ethical relativist) moral judgments are not objectively true or false, but only true or false *for* particular individuals. To say that a statement or judgment is objectively true is to say that it is correct for any rational being to accept it and that anyone who rejects it is mistaken.

The present book focuses on three kinds of questions about the status of morals. (1) What is the correct analysis of the meaning of moral judgments, i.e., what does it mean to say that something is good or bad or right or wrong? (2) In what sense, if any, can moral judgments be said to be correct or incorrect? Is one ever rationally compelled to accept one moral judgment as opposed to another? (3) To what extent do first-order normative judgments presuppose views about the status of the norms in question? Is it consistent for an extreme meta-ethical relativist to make any first-order normative judgments? Do any of our attitudes about the world presuppose views about the status of norms?

Any theory about the meaning of moral judgments has implications for questions regarding their justification and their correctness and incorrectness; and any claim concerning the objectivity of morals presupposes certain views as to the correct analysis of moral concepts. For example, if hedonistic naturalism is true, then at least some moral judgments are objectively true or false and can be known to be such on the basis of empirical observation. Moreover, any denial of the objectivity of morality presupposes the falsity of this and certain other views about the nature of moral judgments. So, questions about the meaning of moral judgments are prior to questions about their objectivity and justification. The priority of questions about meaning is reflected in the organization of the present book. In the first chapter, I shall argue that moral judgments are statements about the correctness or appropriateness of attitudes. This view about the nature of moral judgments, which is derived from Brentano, can be stated roughly as follows: to make a favorable moral judgment about something, to say that it is good or right etc., is to say that it is correct to have a favorable attitude about it. To make an unfavorable moral judgment about something, i.e., to say that it is bad or wrong, etc., is to say that it is correct to have an unfavorable attitude about it. I will argue that this view, which I call 'The Brentanist Theory', is more plausible than any of the standard positions in contemporary Anglo-American moral philosophy — emotivism, prescriptivism, naturalism, and intuitionism. Emotivism and prescriptivism, which are the two most influential non-cognitivist theories, are unable to account for the fact that moral judgments *purport* to be objectively correct, nor can they deal adequately with problems related to moral weakness and moral change. Naturalism and intuitionism fail to account for the emotive import of moral judgments and for the ability of moral considerations to motivate us to act against our instinctive desires. The Brentanist theory combines the virtues of both cognitivism and non-cognitivism. I will argue that it avoids all of the major objections that have been raised against the received positions.

If the Brentanist Theory is true, then in order for there to be objective moral facts in the way that there are objective facts about the physical world there would have to be features of things in virtue of which it is correct (in a sense that is opposed to incorrect) for all rational beings to have a certain sort of attitude about them. For example, if it is a fact that lying is morally wrong, then it must be the case that it is correct for any rational creature to have an unfavorable attitude about lying. It does not, I shall argue, seem to be the case that attitudes can be correct in this strong sense. It follows that moral judgments cannot be correct in the sense that implies that any conceivable rational being who rejects a correct judgment must be mistaken. In Chapter Two, I will argue that these considerations commit us to the view that moral judgments can only be correct in the sense of not being based upon false beliefs or incomplete information etc. This is tantamount to saying that some kind of version of the ideal observer theory is the appropriate standard for determining the correctness or incorrectness of moral judgments. According to the ideal observer theory, a moral judgment about a particular moral issue can be said to be correct, provided that all ideal observers would accept that judgment or have attitudes that correspond to it. (Very roughly a favorable attitude corresponds to a favorable moral judgment and an unfavorable attitude corresponds to an unfavorable moral judgment.)

I will argue that Firth's classic version of the ideal observer theory does not, as he claims, support moral objectivism, but rather an extreme version of meta-ethical relativism according to which there are no objectively correct moral views. For, contrary to what Firth says, all possible ideal observers would not agree in their attitudes about any moral issues. Then, I will propose a revised version of the ideal observer theory. The distinctive features of my view are the following:

(1) I do not require that an ideal observer be disinterested, dispassionate, or "normal".

(2) In addition to knowledge of all of the relevant facts, I require that an ideal observer possess full knowledge of all of the possible moral principles that bear on the issues that he is considering and all of the implications of those principles.

(3) I require that the attitudes of the ideal observer not have been influenced by training or association with people who were ill-informed or who fall short of being ideal observers in other respects.

(4) I hold that anyone whose views or attitudes about something are dependent on his having been mistaken about or ignorant of relevant facts about it at any time in the past should be disqualified as an ideal observer. This amounts to extending the requirement of full information to include full information about all of the things about which one makes one's judgments at all times in the past when one's attitudes were being formed.

(5) I require that the views or attitudes of an ideal observer not involve any kind of 'emotional displacement'. Among other things, this means that a person cannot be an ideal observer if any of his unfavorable attitudes or judgments about things constitute an outlet for pent-up anger aroused by *other sources*. For example, if a person's judgment that we ought to 'nuke' Iran is an outlet for free-floating hostility, he should to that extent be disqualified as an ideal observer. Nietzsche argues that certain normative views should be rejected or discounted because they are expressions or products of *ressentiment* or repressed hostility. I will argue that, given some version of the ideal observer theory, the sorts of genetic arguments that Nietzsche gives are perfectly valid.

(6) I require that the attitudes of ideal observers not involve the kind of self-deception that typically occurs when people take a sour grapes attitude about things that they really want or when they make a virtue out of necessity.

(7) I argue that Firth's requirement that an ideal observer be a human being means that the theory cannot provide us with standards for determining when moral judgments are objectively correct (or correct for all possible rational beings), but at most only standards for determining when moral judgments are true for all human beings.

I shall argue that ideal observers would all agree in their attitudes about some, but not all, moral issues. Therefore, my revised version of the ideal observer theory supports the claim that there are moral judgments that are correct for all human beings concerning some, but not all, moral issues.

In Chapter One, I argue that several of the characteristic functions of moral judgments require that they purport to be correct, at least in the sense of being correct for all human beings. In Chapter Two, I argue that there are many moral issues (probably the vast majority) concerning which there is no moral judgment that is correct for all human beings. I am thus committed to the view that there are many moral issues concerning which any moral judgment is mistaken or false. Judgments about such issues purport to be correct in a sense in which they are not. My view denies much of what is implicit in our ordinary moral claims. Therefore, it is important for me to determine what sorts of uses of morality and what sorts of views and attitudes associated with the moral point of view I am committed to abandoning and also whether the view that I am left with is, in any sense, a moral one. The last two chapters of the book deal with this issue and take up larger questions about the connection between meta-ethical views and first-order moral judgments.

In Chapter Three, I shall argue that moral judgments purport to be correct in a sense in which most standard versions of ethical relativism deny that they are. Therefore, most standard versions of moral relativism are nihilistic views. By this I mean that it is inconsistent for anyone who holds such views to make any first-order moral judgments. However, I shall also argue that the view defended in Chapter Two permits me to make moral judgments, even about those issues concerning which I hold that there is no judgment that is correct for all human beings.

The fourth and final chapter of the book attempts to determine whether any of our ordinary commitments and attitudes about the world presuppose a belief in the objectivity of morals. More specifically, I want to determine whether being a relativist commits one to having the nihilistic attitude of not caring about anything and not valuing some things more than others. I will argue that being a relativist does not commit one to being indifferent about everything; nor does it commit one to revising or abandoning any of one's first-order attitudes or commitments. Granted that the rejection of the objectivity of morals does not logically compel one to revise one's first-order attitudes, there are still many people whose attitudes and commitments are causally dependent on their believing in the objectivity of morality. The rejection of moral objectivism can have a profound effect on a person's life and conduct. The sort of person whose attitudes and commitments are most dependent on his subscribing to objectivist meta-ethical views is one whose instinctive emotions and attitudes are strongly at variance with his moral principles — for example, a person who acts generously simply as a matter of principle without having any emotional inclination to be generous. (Kant's ideal of the morally praiseworthy individual bears some resemblance to this.) Such a person is likely to cease acting in accordance with his principles if he becomes a relativist and no longer believes that those principles are objectively correct. The sort of person whose

instinctive desires are in harmony with his reflective principles
(and who doesn't need to resist his instinctive desires in order to
act in accordance with his principles — Aristotle takes this to be a
requirement for being morally virtuous) is very likely to be someone whose attitudes and commitments are relatively independent
of his views as to the status of the principles that he accepts. His
own natural desires will provide him with reasons to act in accordance with those principles, even if he ceases to believe that the
principles are, in any sense, correct.

CHAPTER ONE

A BRENTANIST THEORY OF MORAL JUDGMENTS

1.1. THE THEORY

1.1.1. *Brentano's Analysis of the Meaning of Moral Judgments*

Brentano's theory about the meaning and nature of moral judgments merits serious consideration as an alternative to the standard theories in contemporary Anglo-American moral philosophy. According to Brentano, moral judgments are statements about the correctness of attitudes:

We call a thing *good* when the love relating to it is correct. In the broadest sense of the term, the good is that which is worthy of love, that which can be loved with a love that is correct.[1]

And when we call certain objects good and bad we are merely saying that whoever loves the former and hates the latter has taken the right stand.[2]

Accordingly, everything that can be thought about belongs in one of two classes — either the class of things for which love is appropriate, or the class of things for which hate is appropriate. Whatever falls into the first class we call good, and whatever falls into the second we call bad.[3]

When we call one good "better" than another, we mean that the one is preferable to the other. In other words, it is *correct to prefer* the one good for its own sake, to the other.[4]

(Strictly speaking, Brentano does not hold that all moral judgments are statements about the correctness of attitudes; on his view judgments about the rightness or wrongness of actions are not statements about the correctness of attitudes. However, according to him, they are derivable from judgments about good

1

and bad which, in turn, are statements about the correctness of attitudes (see below).)

There are other philosophers who hold the weaker view that the assertion of the correctness of certain attitudes is an essential *part* of the meaning of moral judgments. Carl Wellman writes the following:

"This is good" and "no, it is bad" are opposed because, while the former claims implicitly that favor is the rational attitude to take towards the object, the latter claims that disfavor is the rational attitude.[5]

Consider also the following passage from Sidgwick:

Here we are met by the suggestion that the judgments or propositions which we commonly call moral — in the narrow sense — really affirm no more than the existence of a specific emotion in the mind of the person who utters them; that when I say 'Truth ought to be spoken' or 'Truthspeaking is right,' I mean no more than that the idea of truthspeaking excites in my mind a feeling of approbation or satisfaction. . . . If I say that 'the air is sweet,' or 'the food is disagreeable,' it would not be exactly true to say that I mean no more than I like the one or dislike the other; but if my statement is challenged, I shall probably content myself with affirming the existence of such feelings in my own mind. But there appears to me to be a fundamental difference between this case and that of moral feelings. The peculiar emotion of moral approbation is, in my experience, inseparably bound up with the conviction, implicit or explicit, that the conduct approved is 'really' right, i.e., that it cannot without error be disapproved by any other mind.[6]

Brentano holds that moral judgments are or are derivable from statements about the correctness of love and hatred, where 'love' and 'hatred' ('*Lieben*' and '*Hassen*') are taken in the broadest possible sense. He uses the words '*Lieben*' and '*Hassen*' interchangeably with '*Gefallen*' and '*Missfallen*'.[7] The German word '*Gefallen*' means 'pleasure', 'preference', 'choice', or 'favor'. *Gefallen* with an object is a matter both of how one feels about it or is disposed to feel about it and of how one is disposed to act with respect to it; one is disposed to feel pleased with it and to prefer its existence or occurrence to its non-existence or non-occurrence all other things being equal. Brentano distinguishes between choice and preference. A person can have preferences concerning things that are not a matter of choice for him. For example, someone may have a preference that the sun rise in the morning.[8] However, we can still say that a person's preferences are ultimately to be determined by facts about how he would choose in various *hypothetical* situations. For example, to say that someone prefers that the sun rise rather than not is to say that he would choose to have it rise if it were within his power to decide. The analysis of love and hatred ('*Gefallen*' and '*Missfallen*') in terms of both feelings and action tendencies is supported by Brentano's analysis of 'better' as that which it is correct to prefer (*vorziehen*) and the passages in *Psychology From an Empirical Standpoint* in which he says that the phenomena of love and hatred include both feeling and will.[9]

It is quite common for people to have mixed feelings or conflicting attitudes about various things. For example, a married person may have mixed feelings about an opportunity to commit adultery with an attractive member of the opposite sex. We need to find criteria for determining whether a person's attitudes are favorable or unfavorable on the whole in such cases. I suggest the following:

> Whether someone loves or hates something on the whole is ultimately a function of how he is disposed to act. A person who loves something will choose or prefer its existence or occurrence to its non-existence or non-occurrence, all other things being equal, a person who hates something will choose or prefer its non-existence or non-occurrence to its existence or occurrence, all other things being equal.

Let me stress that the above view should not necessarily be attributed to Brentano. My aim in this chapter is not to give an interpretation of Brentano but to construct a plausible theory that derives its inspiration from him.

I shall now attempt to explain what Brentano means by correct and incorrect attitudes. I shall incorporate these notions into my own alternative theory. The German word *'richtig'* is ambiguous in just the same way as the English words 'right' and 'correct' — it may mean right in the sense that is opposed to mistaken or it may mean right in the sense of being proper or morally right. I think that it is clear that Brentano intends the notion of correctness to be understood in the former sense. For it would clearly be circular to define moral concepts in terms of some kind of notion of a proper or morally acceptable attitude. Another reason for accepting the former reading of 'correct' instead of the latter is that Brentano says that attitudes or emotions can be correct or incorrect in just the same sense as ordinary factual judgments. Brentano rejects the correspondence theory of truth. According to him, the truth of a judgment (or the correctness of an attitude) consists not in its corresponding to reality, but rather in its being correct, fitting, or appropriate.[10] He attempts to analyze the notion of correct and incorrect affirmation by reference to the concept of correct and incorrect emotions.[11] Brentano claims that judgments and attitudes are objectively correct or incorrect, i.e., correct for all rational beings. If it is correct for someone to disapprove of cruelty, then it must be correct for any rational being to do so. Brentano's notion of correct and incorrect attitudes is intelligible. We know what it means to say that attitudes can be objectively correct or incorrect. It is quite another thing to explain *how* this could be the case or to show that *it is* the case. These issues will be addressed in Sections 1.4 and 2.1.

1.1.2. *My Own Revised Account — 'The Brentanist Theory'*

Brentano is a 'teleologist', that is, he defines 'right' and 'wrong' (he uses the term 'right end') in terms of the concepts of good and bad. 'Right action' or 'right end' simply means 'the action that results in the best balance of good over bad'.[12] The plausibility of teleological theories of right and wrong is a matter of great controversy. Since we are not in a position to settle these issues here, we ought to formulate the theory so as to avoid a commitment to either teleological or deontological theories. I suggest the following revised version of Brentano's theory:

> To make a favorable moral judgment about something, to say that it is good or right, etc., is to say that it is correct (in a sense that is opposed to mistaken) to have a favorable attitude about it; to make a negative moral judgment about something is to say that it is correct to have an unfavorable attitude about it.

I shall call this the 'Brentanist Theory'. It differs from Brentano's own theory in that (1) it does not commit one to a teleological theory of right and wrong, and (2) it takes the favorableness and unfavorableness of attitudes ('love' and 'hatred') to be ultimately a function of one's action tendencies. As stated, the Brentanist Theory does not provide any way to distinguish between different kinds of favorable and unfavorable moral judgments. It does not, for example, explain the difference between calling something good and calling it right. I shall attempt to show how the theory can be qualified so as to allow a basis for such distinctions in Section 1.4.

Here it might be objected that it can be correct to have a neutral attitude about good things. It is not incorrect for me to fail to be pleased by the news of each good thing that I learn about during the day. I need not, for example, feel pleased each time I learn of a good harvest in some distant land or the safe completion of an airline flight. However, this is not an objection to my theory. When I say that it would be incorrect to be indifferent to what is good I am only claiming that it would be incorrect for one not to have some kind of minimal preference for the occurrence or existence of the good things. If it is good that an airplane doesn't crash, then it is incorrect for one to prefer that the plane crash rather than land safely, other things being equal. Similar remarks apply to the notions of badness and wrongness. It is not incorrect for one to fail to feel displeased about every bit of bad news that one learns during the course of the day. However, other things being equal, it is incorrect not to prefer the non-existence or non-occurrence of what is bad.

I shall now propose a Brentanist analysis of the concept of being morally indifferent. To say that something is morally indifferent is not to say that it is correct (in a sense that is opposed to mistaken) to be indifferent to it. To say that something is morally indifferent is to imply that it would be correct to be indifferent to it, but it does not imply that favorable or unfavorable attitudes are incorrect. When I say that watching the World Series is morally indifferent I mean that it can be correct to have a favorable, unfavorable or neutral attitude about it. Calling x morally indifferent doesn't mean that we are committed to being indifferent about it, rather it means that it is a matter of indifference what kind of attitude we have about it.

It might be objected that there are cases in which it is incorrect to have an unfavorable attitude about something that is morally indifferent. Isn't it incorrect to have an unfavorable attitude about such things as a person's skin color? I would contend that there is nothing incorrect or inappropriate about such an attitude – no more than it is incorrect to prefer shirts of a certain color to those of other colors. The reason that we are inclined to think that the dislike of a certain skin color is incorrect is that it is usually associated with other kinds of attitudes and desires that are incorrect, e.g., an unfavorable attitude about the happiness or welfare of individuals of that skin color, or the preference that their interests be subordinated to those of members of other groups. In and of itself, a dislike of such things as black skin, red hair, or a squeaky voice is morally beyond reproach. Similarly, it can be correct to be either favorably, unfavorably or indifferently disposed towards actions that are morally indifferent. However, it is incorrect to wish someone ill on account of his having done something that is morally indifferent.

Supererogatory actions count as morally indifferent according to the present classification. They are neither wrong nor obligatory. On my view it can be correct for one to be indifferent or ill-disposed to such actions. This might seem to be an objectionable consequence. But I think not. For to deny that it can be correct for the agent or someone else to prefer that he not perform the action in question is tantamount to denying that it is permissible for him not to do it. It is not, for example, necessarily incorrect for a man and his family to prefer that he not make a martyr of himself, rather than sacrifice himself for the sake of some greater good. Surely some kind of favorable attitude is in order when someone performs a supererogatory act. It is correct in a sense that is opposed to mistaken to have a favorable attitude about the agent and his character, but it is not correct in a sense that is opposed to mistaken to have a favorable attitude about the act itself. Supererogatory acts are acts in virtue of which a person can be said to be morally praiseworthy. It is incorrect to fail to have a favorable attitude about those aspects of a person's character that cause him to perform supererogatory acts. (See Section 1.4.2.)

According to my theory, moral judgments assert the correctness or incorrectness of certain attitudes. This can be illustrated by means of the following chart:

	Incorrect	Correct
(1) x is good (obligatory, etc.)	un	f
(2) x is bad (wrong, etc.)	fn	u
(3) x is morally indifferent (neither good nor bad nor right nor wrong)		fnu

f = a favorable attitude.
n = a neutral attitude.
u = an unfavorable attitude.

Column II includes all attitudes that it is correct (in the sense of not being mistaken) for one to have. Thus, any kind of attitude about anything must be either correct or incorrect in this present sense. To say that an attitude is correct in this sense is not necessarily to imply that any other kind of attitude is mistaken.

The notions depicted here do not exhaust all of the possibilities. Consider also the following:

	Incorrect	Correct
(4)	fnu	
(5)	n	fu
(6)	u	fn
(7)	f	nu
(8)	fu	n

As this makes clear, our ordinary moral concepts do not even begin to exhaust all of the possible claims that one could make about the correctness of attitudes concerning something. Let us

consider these additional possibilities in order. There is no predicate corresponding to line 4. There is no term in the English
language that we can apply to something to indicate that any
attitude concerning it is mistaken. Indeed, it seems clear that
such a notion is incoherent. To say that an attitude is incorrect
is to say that one is in error in holding that particular attitude
as opposed to some other. If an attitude about something is
mistaken then there must be another attitude that is not mistaken.
(To say that an attitude is mistaken is to say that one is mistaken
in holding that particular attitude as opposed to another that is
not mistaken.) There is no single term that captures the idea
incorporated in line 5. However, this notion is familiar enough.
Sometimes those who say that one must either be "for or against"
something can be taken to mean that it is correct to have either
a favorable or unfavorable attitude about it, but incorrect to be
indifferent. There are no things concerning which I would be
prepared to make such a claim. However, I think that it is at
least conceivable that there could be something that it is correct
to be for or against but incorrect for one to be indifferent towards. Much the same kinds of remarks apply to lines 6 and 7.
They do not correspond to any of our ordinary moral notions.
(Some might contend that they correspond to the notions of
good and bad. However, as I argued earlier, it is incorrect to be
completely indifferent to what is good (obligatory) or bad
(wrong).) There is nothing concerning which I would be prepared
to claim that it can be correct to have either a neutral or favorable
attitude about it but incorrect to have an unfavorable attitude.
Nor am I prepared to claim of anything that it is correct to have a
neutral or unfavorable attitude about it, but incorrect to have a
favorable attitude. However, I am not certain that there is nothing
concerning which such claims could be correctly made.

    To say that it is correct to be indifferent to something (and
incorrect to have any other kind of attitude about it) is equivalent

to saying that attitudes about it are correct or incorrect in the way illustrated in line 8. I know of no reasons for thinking that we are committed to being indifferent to anything. Moreover there are reasons for supposing that it is false that there is anything about which indifference is the only correct attitude. For the claim that there is anything concerning which indifference is the only correct attitude conflicts with the following principle, which I take to be *prima facie* plausible: if it is correct to be indifferent to something then it must also be correct to have a favorable attitude about it. (I call this the non-killjoy principle.) If this principle is true then it also follows that there is nothing such that attitudes concerning it are correct and incorrect as depicted in line 7.

I shall attempt to defend the Brentanist Theory in the rest of this chapter. Even if successful, my arguments fall short of conclusively establishing its truth. I shall only argue that the Brentanist theory is more plausible than the most familiar alternative theories about the nature and meaning of moral judgments. In Sections 1.2 and 1.3, I shall present some objections to the four standard views about the nature of moral judgments in contemporary Anglo-American moral philosophy — emotivism, prescriptivism, naturalism and intuitionism — and argue that the Brentanist Theory avoids all of these objections.

In Section 1.4, I shall attempt to defend the Brentanist Theory against a number of possible objections.

1.2. GROUNDS FOR PREFERRING THE BRENTANIST THEORY TO THE STANDARD NON-COGNITIVIST THEORIES

1.2.1. Cognitivism and Non-Cognitivism

It is customary to classify theories about the nature of moral judgments as either cognitivist or non-cognitivist. Cognitivism is the view that moral judgments are statements that are either true or false in just the same sense in which ordinary non-moral judgments such as 'grass is green' are true or false. Non-cognitivism is the view that moral judgments are not statements that are either true or false. The two most important non-cognitivist theories in contemporary Anglo-American philosophy are emotivism and prescriptivism. In its crudest form emotivism is the view that moral judgments are nothing more than expressions of attitudes such as 'Boo Beria'.[13] More sophisticated versions of emotivism such as those proposed by Ayer and Stevenson only imply that the statement or expression of attitudes is *part* of the meaning of moral judgments (see below). Hare, who is the most important proponent of prescriptivism and from whom the term is derived, holds that moral judgments are tantamount to commands or requests such as 'close the door' or 'be quiet!' They differ from ordinary commands or requests only in that they are "universalizable" and "overriding" (see below).

1.2.2. Emotivism

The crude version of emotivism according to which the meaning of moral judgments consists solely in the expression of emotions or attitudes is generally conceded to be untenable. (See Section 1.2.3.) Because of this, emotivists have come to hold that the meaning of moral judgments consists only partly in the expression of attitudes. Ayer, for example, says that it is another aspect of the meaning of moral judgments that they are intended to affect the attitudes and actions of other people.[14] So, on Ayer's view, to make a moral judgment is to express an attitude with the intention of influencing the attitudes or actions of other people. Stevenson agrees with Ayer that moral judgments have "dynamic meaning", i.e., it is a part of their meaning that they can be used to influence the attitudes of other people. However, Stevenson holds that moral judgments involve statements asserting the existence of attitudes rather than expressions of attitudes. According to him, 'x is good' means roughly, " 'I approve of x; do so as well'."[15]

1.2.3. Emotivism and Moral Disagreement

It is almost universally conceded that the existence of moral disagreements is a serious problem for emotivism.[16] Consider a paradigm case of a moral dispute. One person holds that Stalin was a good man and another holds that he was a bad man. If one of the crude versions of emotivism were true, that is, if moral judgments were nothing more than expressions of or statements about one's attitudes, then this could not constitute a disagreement. For we would not be disagreeing if I said that I liked him and you said that you disliked him. Nor would we be disagreeing if I expressed a favorable attitude by cheering at the mention of his name and you hissed. The theories of Ayer and Stevenson appear to be considerably more plausible in such cases. Stevenson and Ayer would say that the disagreement in the present case consists in the fact that each person is attempting to alter the attitudes of the other.[17] But for reasons I shall give below this is not a satisfactory account of the nature of moral disagreement. It is an essential aspect of such disputes that each of the two parties believes that the other's attitudes are in some sense incorrect or mistaken. (See Sections 1.2.5 and 1.2.10 below and Chapter Three.) The Brentanist Theory offers a most plausible account of the nature of ethical disagreement that accounts for this essential feature of moral disputes. According to the Brentanist Theory, a disagreement between two people about the moral status of x consists in their disagreeing about what attitudes it is correct to have about x.

1.2.4. Can Emotivism Explain the Difference Between Moral Judgments and Non-Moral Judgments?

Emotivism does not provide a satisfactory basis for distinguishing between moral judgments and other sorts of judgments or expressions of attitudes. Suppose that there are three people, *A*, *B*, and *C*, in an ice cream shop and that *A* and *B* are tasting a particular flavor of ice cream. *A* says to *C*, "Umm, this is good, try it". *B* says to *C*, "Ugh, it's awful, try something else". It is difficult to see how Ayer and Stevenson can avoid the absurd consequence that *A* and *B* are making moral judgments – they are each expressing attitudes about the ice cream and each is trying to influence *C*'s behavior. Here it might be suggested that moral judgments are distinguishable from other sorts of expressions of favorable and unfavorable attitudes in that they involve the expression of distinctively moral kinds of attitudes. Favorable moral judgments involve the expression of attitudes of moral approval or moral approbation; unfavorable moral judgments involve the expression of moral disapprobation.[18] However, moral approbation and disapprobation are not distinguishable from other sorts of favorable and unfavorable attitudes in the way required in order for this reply to succeed. According to most views, moral approval and disapproval are distinguishable from other sorts of favorable and unfavorable attitudes only in virtue of their etiology. Approval and disapproval are favorable and unfavorable attitudes that one has as a result of having made favorable or unfavorable moral judgments. There are no other reasonable ways of distinguishing between moral approval and other sorts of favorable and unfavorable attitudes. Approval and disapproval do not involve any special 'feelings' or phenomenological properties that are unique to them. Nor is it plausible to distinguish approval and disapproval by any special intentional properties or behavioral dispositions that they manifest. It seems that approval and disapproval can be distinguished from other sorts of attitudes only in virtue of having come about as a result of one's accepting moral judgments. This means that the concept of a moral judgment is logically prior to the concept of moral approbation and disapprobation. From this it follows that the emotivist cannot distinguish between moral judgments and expressions of other kinds of attitudes (and thus meet the objection) by appealing to the notions of approval and disapproval.

Another line of response to this criticism is suggested by the following passage from Stevenson's *Ethics and Language* in which he says that:

The emotive meaning of a word is the power that the word acquires, on account of its history in emotional situations, to evoke or directly express attitudes . . . .[19]

It might be suggested that we can distinguish 'x is a good man' from 'x is a good flavor of ice cream' on the grounds that the former has a greater or stronger emotive meaning — it has a greater power to affect the attitudes and conduct of other people and/or it expresses stronger attitudes. However, the proposed account of emotive meaning is quite implausible. According to this view, the emotive meaning of such words as 'good' and 'duty' consists in their power to influence people's emotions and behavior and express attitudes. This is surely not a correct theory of emotive meaning. For suppose that all people became amoral, i.e., indifferent to moral considerations. Moral terms would lose their causal power and when used would not express strong attitudes, but they would still have the same meaning as before.

The Brentanist Theory provides a very plausible account of the difference between moral judgments and judgments of taste. A judgment of taste is simply a statement about the existence of a preference or an attitude. A moral judgment asserts the correctness of such a preference or attitude. The essential difference between saying 'this is a good flavor of ice cream' and 'Quisling was a bad man' is that in the latter case I am implying that it is correct or fitting to disapprove of Quisling and that anyone who has a favorable attitude about him is mistaken. When I say that this is a good flavor of ice cream I do not presume that it would be incorrect for someone else not to like it. I allow for the possibility that it may be perfectly correct for others not to like it.

1.2.5. *Emotivism Cannot Give a Satisfactory Account of What Happens When People Change Their Views About Moral Questions*

An important part of our ordinary moral views is that we often regard our own attitudes or actions as incorrect or mistaken. The kind of case that best illustrates this is one in which a person undergoes swift and radical changes in his moral beliefs without undergoing any comparable changes in attitude. The emotivist theory is unable to account for such cases. Suppose that a young man with extremely puritanical views about sexual morality reads Bertrand Russell's *Marriage and Morals* and, accepting the arguments there, comes to believe that 'anything goes between consenting adults'. It is very unlikely that his attitudes about sex will change very suddenly. He may still be disgusted by such things as homosexuality and casual sex and have strong feelings against people who engage in such activities. He may still also be strongly disinclined to participate in those acts himself and still be disposed to feel very guilty just for thinking about them. His overall attitude about all forms of sex other than the standard positions within marriage is still decidedly negative. The only thing that permits us to say that his views about sexual morality have changed (and changed completely) is that he no longer believes that his attitudes about sex are correct — he believes that they are incorrect and irrational.

There are other difficulties for the emotivist that arise in cases
in which people change their views about moral questions. Suppose that at time t I say that x is right and then at a later time,
t', I say that x is wrong. According to the emotivist, all that has
happened is that I have changed my attitudes about x; I now
disapprove of x and want to cause others to have negative attitudes about it. But surely there is more to it than this. When
I say that x is wrong at t' I am not just reporting a change of
attitude and/or a change in my intentions with respect to influencing the attitudes of others. I am saying that my previous
attitude was incorrect and that it has been rectified.[20] In this
context it is instructive to contrast moral change with change
of taste. I used to hate cantaloupes and now I like them, but
I have no inclination to say that my taste has been corrected.[21]

1.2.6. According to Emotivism a Favorable (Unfavorable) Moral Judgment About Something Is Insincere Unless One Has a Favorable (Unfavorable) Attitude About It

According to emotivism, any moral judgment concerning x involves either (a) a statement about one's attitudes concerning x,
or (b) the expression of an attitude about x. Emotivism also
implies that moral judgments state or express determinate kinds
of attitudes. A favorable moral judgment must state or express a
favorable attitude, an unfavorable moral judgment must state or
express an unfavorable attitude. All versions of emotivism imply
that a moral judgment is insincere unless one actually has the
attitude that the judgment purports to state or express. For
instance, an emotivist must say that my judgment that St. Paul
was a bad man is insincere unless I have an unfavorable attitude
about him.

1.2.7. Prescriptivism Denies the Possibility of Moral Weakness

The most influential non-cognitivist analysis of moral judgments other than emotivism is the view defended by R. M. Hare in *The Language of Morals*, *Freedom and Reason*, and *Moral Thinking*.[22] Hare's view is commonly referred to as 'prescriptivism'. The analysis of the meaning of moral judgments defended in *The Language of Morals* is that moral judgments are 'universalizable prescriptions'.[23] Moral judgments are prescriptions or imperatives on the order of 'shut the door' or 'stop!' They are distinguishable from other sorts of imperatives in that they are "universalizable". This means that a person who makes a moral judgment about something is committed to making exactly the same judgment about anything that is similar to it in the relevant respects.[24] This view fails to provide an adequate basis for distinguishing between moral judgments and other sorts of prescriptions, e.g., 'don't bet on a lame horse'. This latter sort of prescription could be universalizable in Hare's sense. In *Freedom and Reason* and *Moral Thinking* Hare avoids this problem by adding the condition that moral judgments must be "overriding".[25] To say that moral judgments must be overriding means that the prescriptions expressed in moral judgments must override other prescriptions in cases of conflict. 'Don't bet on a lame horse' (as said by me) is not a moral judgment, because I would be willing to have it overridden by my moral principles if there were cases of conflict. According to Hare, accepting a moral judgment entails assenting to a prescription. For example, accepting the moral judgment that killing is wrong entails assenting to the prescription 'don't kill'. Hare says that in order for one to be said to "assent to" a prescription (or an overriding prescription) it is necessary that one follow it (whenever possible).[26] This is tantamount to a denial of the existence of moral weakness in the ordinary sense. (This, itself, I take to be a decisive objection to Hare's theory, although he struggles forthrightly with the problem — see *Freedom and Reason*, Chapter 5.) According to Hare, if a person fails to do something that he professes to believe he ought to do, then it follows that either he was unable to do it or that he didn't really believe that he ought to do it.

1.2.8. *Prescriptivism and Emotivism Are Unable to Account for the Fact that There Are People Who Are Completely Indifferent to Moral Considerations (Amoralists)*

I consider it to be a fatal objection to both emotivism and prescriptivism that there are people who are almost completely indifferent to moral considerations (amoralists) and individuals who are moved by anti-moral considerations (immoralists). Some people sincerely accept moral principles or moral judgments without having any inclination to act on them or disapprove of those who fail to do so. I have heard people make statements of the sort 'I know that I ought to do such and such but I just don't care' in cases in which I had no reason to doubt their sincerity. It might be argued that such individuals are using moral terms in an inverted commas sense. When a person says that x is wrong but he doesn't care, he simply means that x is contrary to conventional moral standards and that he doesn't care about *that*. He doesn't think that x is "really" wrong — if he did he couldn't be indifferent about its being wrong. Such cases, however, cannot always be described in this way. For there are cases in which a person says that he knows that something is right or wrong but just doesn't care when he knows that his judgment is contrary to conventional standards, which would suggest that he "really" believes that x is right or wrong. For example, a person may believe that it is wrong to eat meat but just not care. There are a great many people who are indifferent or relatively indifferent to moral considerations. At least some of them have genuine beliefs or convictions about moral questions. Ordinary people can become relatively indifferent to moral considerations under the grip of intense emotions — love, hatred, anger, and despair, etc., but they do not necessarily lose their convictions or beliefs about moral questions in such circumstances.

I should stress that being an amoralist in the sense that I am concerned with here is different from being a moral nihilist or a moral skeptic. An amoralist is someone who grants the existence or validity of moral considerations but is indifferent to them. A moral nihilist denies the existence or validity of moral consider-ations — he denies that anything is right or wrong or good or bad. Moral skeptics doubt the existence of moral considerations. Here, it is well to note a difference in terminology. In *Moral Thinking*, Hare uses the term 'amoral' to refer to someone who doesn't accept any moral judgments (p. 112). I would call such a person either a nihilist or a skeptic. Hare allows for the possibility that there could be amoralists in his sense of the word. However, as I have argued, on his view it is logically impossible that there could be an amoralist in my sense of the term.

1.2.9. *Prescriptivism and Emotivism Are Unable to Account for the Fact that There Are People Who Are Moved by Anti-Moral Considerations (Immoralists)*

An equally serious problem for emotivism and prescriptivism is the case of the immoralist — someone who loves evil and hates good for their own sake. Other things being equal, an immoralist is more favorably disposed towards something if he thinks that it is bad or evil and he is less favorably disposed towards it if he thinks that it is right or good. The emotivist and prescriptivist might offer the same sort of reply considered earlier and say that the immoralist who appears to be making moral judgments is merely using moral terms in an inverted commas sense.[27] A person may love what is thought to be wrong or evil according to conventional standards, but it is logically impossible to love something because (one thinks that) it is "really" evil. No doubt this analysis is a correct account of most ostensible cases of the love of evil. Most of those who are attracted to certain unusual forms of sexual activity because they are 'wicked' simply get some kind of titillation from flaunting conventional morality (or being thought by others to flaunt conventional morality). However, the love of evil sometimes attains a sinister and demonic character that indicates more than a mere flaunting of conventional standards, but rather a flaunting of standards that one takes to be correct, oneself. It is not difficult to give a plausible psychological picture of an immoralist. An immoralist might be someone who desires to be perverse, i.e., have incorrect attitudes. Anyone who had such desires to the degree that they were not always overridden by opposing desires would count as an immoralist in a sense that non-cognitivists cannot allow for. Non-cognitivists cannot account for the fact that people sometimes do things for the sake of being morally perverse. The desire to be perverse could be a result of hostility towards figures of authority such as one's parents or a result of unpleasant associations with early moral training. The evident delight that many people take in being perverse suggests that they do have such desires. Some of the great villains of fiction, e.g., Richard III and Milton's Satan are likely cases of the love of evil.[28] I do not wish to insist upon the claim that immoralists actually exist. I do, however, insist on the *conceptual possibility* of such individuals. The sort of love of evil that is often attributed to Satan is perfectly conceivable.

The Brentanist Theory is perfectly able to allow for the possible existence of amoralists and immoralists. According to the Brentanist Theory, the amoralist who says that x is wrong but just doesn't care is indifferent to x but believes that his indifference is incorrect or inappropriate. The immoralist who is attracted to what he thinks is evil because it is evil regards his attitudes as incorrect and may even delight in their being incorrect. Further support for the Brentanist Theory can be found by considering the following case. Suppose that a person says that he believes that x is wrong but that this is a matter of total indifference to him. Suppose also that he does not regard his attitude as being in any sense inappropriate or incorrect. In that case, I think that we would, as the Brentanist Theory suggests, doubt whether he really thinks that x is wrong.

1.2.10. Non-Cognitivist Views Cannot Account for the Fact that Moral Judgments Purport to Be Objectively Correct

Another strong reason for preferring the Brentanist Theory to both emotivism and prescriptivism is that it accounts for the fact that moral judgments *purport* to be objectively correct. If either emotivism or prescriptivism were true, then in making a moral judgment one would not necessarily be implying that the judgment is objectively true, i.e., that any conflicting judgment is mistaken. An emotivist who holds that a certain action is wrong cannot say that those who believe that it is permissible are mistaken, provided that their judgments express the appropriate sorts of attitudes. Similarly, Hare cannot say that those who disagree with him about specific moral issues are mistaken, so long as they "assent to" the prescriptions entailed by their judgments. Perhaps the non-cognitivist could say that moral judgments purport to be correct in the sense of not being based on any false beliefs, but this still allows for the possibility that conflicting judgments could be correct in the same sense. Morality and moral judgments serve a number of important social functions. Among other things they can be used to prescribe or recommend actions and attitudes to other people. I will argue that moral judgments are able to serve all of their characteristic functions only because they *purport* to be objectively correct in a sense in which non-cognitivists deny that they are or even purport to be.

Moral judgments have what Stevenson calls "dynamic meaning".[29] Not only do they typically express one's own attitudes, they can also be used to prescribe or recommend these same attitudes to others. For example, when two people dispute over some moral question, each is trying to persuade the other to adopt his own views. Moral judgments can have this function only in virtue of the fact that they purport to be objectively correct. When I say that S ought to do x I cannot be prescribing that others adopt the same views or attitudes if I am prepared to say in the same breath that it would be correct for them to hold conflicting views. In order to possess the kind of dynamic meaning that Stevenson describes, the moral judgment '_____ is wrong' must not only be taken to imply that it is correct for the speaker to accept this judgment, it must be taken to imply that it would be *correct for anyone* (or at least any human being) to accept it.

Moral judgments are often used to recommend views to others and in order to have this function they must be taken to imply that it is *correct for those to whom they are recommended* to adopt them. This shows that there are instances in which moral judgments assert something more than mere subjective correctness, i.e., their correctness for the speaker. But it does not show that they purport to be objectively correct in the strong sense of implying that it would be correct for anyone to hold them. In order to establish this one would have to show that in making a moral judgment one is prescribing that *everyone else* accept it. This assumption is debatable and I cannot demonstrate it beyond all reasonable doubt. The following remarks must suffice. To debate or dispute with another person about a moral issue is to prescribe that he adopt one's own views and when one makes a moral judgment one is typically prepared to defend it and argue for it against anyone or any other *human being*. Of course, there are situations in which people are fearful of revealing their views about moral issues. For example, members of a totalitarian society may be fearful of expressing views critical of their government to anyone other than trusted friends. However, we can still say — and I believe that this is all that one needs to say — that, for any person whose views about moral issues conflict with one's own, there are some conceivable situations in which one would be willing to defend and recommend one's own views to him.

According to Hare, all moral judgments prescribe actions. This position is somewhat dubious. It is not at all clear that every statement of the form 'x is better than y' implies 'choose x over y all other things being equal'. (Among other things, Hare's view seems to imply that it is necessarily true that an act that has better results than any of its alternatives is morally right or morally obligatory.) In any case, however, there are a great many moral judgments that do prescribe actions. Judgments of the sort 'you ought to do x' and 'it would be wrong for you to do y' are clearly prescriptive. Statements of general principle about right and wrong or duty and obligation also prescribe actions. Given the 'universalizability principle' all moral judgments about the rightness or wrongness of particular actions (including third person judgments and judgments about past actions) are prescriptive. For instance, given that moral judgments are 'universalizable' the judgment 'it was his duty to tell his boss the truth' implies 'tell your boss the truth in any situation like that'.

The prescriptive meaning of moral judgments is dependent on their purporting to be objectively correct or at least correct for all human beings. Suppose that a non-cognitivist tells me that I ought to give blood to the Red Cross and I ask him if it would be correct or equally correct to say that I have no obligation to give blood. To this he replies "Yes and No. It would be incorrect for *me* to say you have no duty to give blood but it would be correct for some other people to say that you have no such duty."

This reply deprives the original judgment of whatever prescriptive force it may once have possessed. This is even more clear if we suppose that he answers by saying "it would be incorrect *for me* to say that you have no duty to give blood but it would be correct *for you* to say that you have no such duty." At the very least, your judgment that *S* ought to do *x* cannot prescribe that he do *x* unless it implies that it would also be correct for him to accept the same judgment.

Contrary to what some cynics say, moral judgments and moral considerations have a considerable influence on human affairs; they often influence people's attitudes and actions. It is doubtful that they could have this kind of causal efficacy unless they *purported* to be objectively correct. Why, for example, should an employer's judgment that racial discrimination is wrong cause him to end discriminatory practices in his place of business unless he took it to imply that his previous attitudes were incorrect?

1.3. GROUNDS FOR PREFERRING THE BRENTANIST THEORY TO THE STANDARD COGNITIVIST THEORIES

1.3.1. *Cognitivist Theories Avoid the Problems Discussed in Sections 1.2.3 and 1.2.4*

As we have seen, emotivism and prescriptivism are open to a number of serious objections that the Brentanist Theory manages to avoid. However, the Brentanist Theory is not the only one that deals adequately with these problems. Indeed it is clear that both of the standard cognitivist theories, naturalism and intuitionism, also avoid all of the objections presented in the preceding part of this chapter. However, as I shall now argue, cognitivist theories are themselves subject to serious objections that the Brentanist Theory avoids. Naturalism, intuitionism, and other familiar versions of cognitivism imply that to make a moral judgment about something, to say that it is good or bad or right or wrong, is to ascribe a quality to it. On this view, moral judgments are true or false in just the same way as ordinary subject-predicate sentences. The statement that grass is green is true if and only if grass has the property of being green. Similarly, the moral judgment that killing is wrong is true if and only if killing possesses the characteristic of being wrong. The Brentanist Theory can, itself, be construed as a cognitivist view. We could say that the judgment that x is wrong is true if and only if x has the property of being such that it is correct for everyone to have an unfavorable attitude about it. I am not sure that I would like my own view to be described as a cognitivist one, but the Brentanist Theory can be read in this way. So, the criticisms of cognitivist theories that follow should not be taken to apply to those cognitivist theories that define moral concepts in terms of the correctness of attitudes.

1.3.2. Cognitivist Theories Cannot Account for the Practical and Emotive Force of Moral Judgments

As many other philosophers have also argued, cognitivist views cannot account for the emotive force of moral judgments or for their ability to provide people with reasons for action.[30] If the nature of moral judgments were as the cognitivist claimed, then it would be difficult to see how moral considerations could have any practical import. If, as the cognitivist says, an action's being wrong *simply consists* in its possessing some descriptive property (a *sui generis* non-natural property, the property of being contrary to God's will or the property of resulting in a greater balance of pleasure over pain than any other course of action open to one, etc.), then there would be no reason to think that its being wrong gave one any reason not to do it. A moral nihilist could accept a descriptivist analysis of moral judgments without making any concessions to the moral point of view. Assume, for example, that a nihilist came to accept a version of hedonistic naturalism according to which 'right action' means the same as 'the act that results in the greatest net balance of pleasure over pain for all sentient creatures'. The nihilist (or former nihilist if you prefer) would then be committed to saying that certain acts are morally right and others morally wrong. But if he takes moral judgments to be purely descriptive, he need not take them to provide him with reasons for doing certain things or for having any particular kinds of attitudes. For it is possible that he has no desire to cause other creatures pleasure or to reduce their suffering. According to the hedonistic naturalist we will have justified certain moral judgments to the nihilist. But this is surely not the case. In order to succeed in justifying a moral judgment to someone it is necessary that he acknowledge that moral considerations have some legitimate claim on his actions and attitudes. A person who denies that moral considerations give him any reasons for viewing things with either favor or disfavor cannot be said to accept any moral judgments.

It is perfectly possible for a person to acknowledge the existence of moral facts in the sense that they are claimed to exist by the cognitivist without conceding that these facts *in any sense* compel people to act in certain ways or compel them to have certain kinds of attitudes. Consider another example. The hedonistic naturalist may convince a nihilistic mass-murderer that 'wrong action' means 'an act of the sort that does not maximize the net hedonic balance' and, therefore, that what he does is wrong in this sense. But unless the mass-murderer concedes that this counts as a reason for ceasing his activities and viewing them with disfavor, we can't say that he believes killing is wrong in the ordinary sense of the word 'wrong'. (This same argument applies to other versions of cognitivism.)

My argument can be summarized as follows:

(1)   Accepting morality or moral judgments implies that one believe that moral considerations have some legitimate claim on one. (For example, to accept the judgment that an act is wrong entails that one recognize that one has reasons not to do it and to view its performance with disfavor.)

(2)   One *could* accept moral judgments in the sense that they are claimed to be true by the standard cognitivist positions, without conceding that they give one reason to do anything or view anything with either favor or disfavor.

Therefore,

(3)   The standard cognitivist views are mistaken.

Premise (2) rests on the assumption that a person *could be* utterly indifferent to those characteristics and states of affairs in terms of which the cognitivist defines moral concepts. I do not need to claim that anyone actually is completely indifferent to them.

While many people may be indifferent to the mysterious characteristics in terms of which intuitionists define moral concepts, few are indifferent to the characteristics in terms of which naturalists define moral notions. For example, most people have at least a minimal desire to promote the general welfare, other things being equal. If we were to become hedonistic naturalists most of us would take the claim that an act is wrong in the sense of being harmful to the general happiness to provide us with some reason not to do it. But such a person would not necessarily be any more motivated to act benevolently if he accepted moral judgments in the way that hedonistic naturalism commits one to accepting them than if he had no moral beliefs at all. His acceptance of this view would not give him any further motivation to act benevolently over and above natural sympathy and concern for the welfare of others. If cognitivism were true it would be difficult to see how morality could serve the objective of compensating for our limited sympathies.[31] It is clear that morality can serve this function. The person of limited sympathies who becomes a utilitarian usually extends the range of his benevolent actions. This could not be the case if people were naturalists. If people took 'right action' to mean nothing more than 'action that best promotes the general welfare', then becoming a utilitarian could not give them any motivations that they did not already have. The fact that moral judgments can serve to compensate for our limited sympathies presupposes at least part of what the Brentanist Theory says. It presupposes that moral judgments are or imply claims about the correctness of attitudes, which means we take moral considerations to give us reasons for discounting or overriding our instinctive desires and inclinations.

In rejecting the standard versions of cognitivism I do not wish to deny the ethical significance of many of the natural and non-natural characteristics of things. Nor do I wish to deny that something may be good or bad or right or wrong *in virtue of* its descriptive characteristics. I am only saying that a thing's *being* good or bad or right or wrong does not *consist* simply in its possessing certain descriptive characteristics.

The Brentanist Theory does full justice to the emotive and practical import of moral judgments. On this view moral judgments are statements about the correctness of emotions and preferences. To say that one thing is better than another is to say that it is correct to prefer it to the other. To say that an action is wrong is to say that it is correct to view it with disfavor and to prefer its non-performance to its performance. To say that a person ought to do something is to say that he would be motivated to do it and to view not doing it with disfavor if his attitudes were correct. Believing that one ought to do something does not require that one have reasons or desires that motivate one to do it, but it does require that one believe that one's attitudes are in some way mistaken or inappropriate if one is not so motivated.

1.3.3. Intuitionist Theories such as Moore's Are Unintelligible Unless Understood in Terms of Something like the Brentanist Theory

Some intuitionists such as Moore hold that moral characteristcs are or are reducible to *sui generis* non-natural properties.[32] As stated, Moore's view is unintelligible. How are we to distinguish the qualities of good and bad? How can we be sure that the characteristic that I intuit and call 'goodness' isn't what you call 'badness'? How can we distinguish between moral qualities and other sorts or non-natural qualities? Moore's theory is intelligible only if it is revised along the lines of Brentano's Theory. The claim that goodness and badness are *sui generis* non-natural properties is intelligible only if we take it to mean something like the following:

> The characteristics of things in virtue of which it is correct to have favorable or unfavorable attitudes about them are *sui generis* non-natural properties.

I do not accept the above principle. However, it is consistent with the Brentanist Theory.

1.3.4. The Brentanist Theory Implies that the Question 'Is It Rational to Be Moral?' Makes No Sense

The implications of the Brentanist Theory concerning questions about the connection between morality and rationality differ from those of the standard cognitivist theories. The Brentanist Theory implies that if there are any correct moral judgments then it is a

mistake to be indifferent to moral considerations. For instance,
if it is in any sense true or correct to say that it is wrong to lie
then the Brentanist Theory implies that it is a mistake or an error
for one to be indifferent to this. The standard cognitivist theories, however, allow for the possibility that it could be perfectly
rational for one to be indifferent to the fact that lying is morally
wrong in some objective sense. Pritchard to the contrary, cognitivist theories leave open the question of whether we have any
reasons for being moral.[33] The Brentanist Theory, however,
implies that if there are any moral facts or correct moral judgments, then one has reasons for being moral (acting morally).
One has reasons for being moral in the following sense. To say
that a certain action is morally objectionable is to say that, if
one's attitudes were correct, then one would be disinclined to
do it oneself and would view other people who do it with disfavor.[34] Here one might ask the question, 'why should I care
about the fact that I would do ____ if my attitudes were correct?'
This is tantamount to asking, 'why should I be rational?' or 'why
should I do the rational thing for me to do?' The Brentanist
Theory does not provide us with any ready justification of rationality. It only implies that there is a connection between being
rational and being moral.

1.3.5. Some Criticisms of Foot's Version of Cognitivism

The arguments that I have presented here apply only to what
might be called 'pure descriptivist' views, i.e., views according to
which moral properties are completely reducible to descriptive
properties. There are weaker versions of descriptivism according
to which moral terms have both descriptive and non-descriptive
meaning. The most notable of these is the view set forth by Foot
in her papers, 'Moral Beliefs' and 'Moral Arguments'.[35] According
to Foot, moral terms have both descriptive and evaluative or

commendatory meaning. The descriptive meaning of moral judgments consists in the fact that moral terms such as 'good' and
'bad' and 'right' and 'wrong' stand in an "internal relationship"
to the objects to which they are applied. By this she means that
there are definite limits to the things to which moral predicates
can be consistently ascribed. For example, Foot holds that something can be called a "good action" only if it satisfies one of the
following conditions: (i) it is the fulfillment of a special duty
derived from a role or promise, or (ii) it exemplifies a virtue.[36]
Among other things, this means that we can't say that twiddling
one's thumbs is a morally good action in the absence of any
special reasons for thinking that it serves some purpose. The evaluative meaning of moral terms consists in the fact that they express attitudes and can be used to commend or induce actions.[37]

Foot notes that many English terms have this kind of dual
meaning — such words as 'rude', 'courage', and 'nigger'. It seems
to me that Foot is simply mistaken about the meaning of our
ordinary moral concepts. Even in the absence of any special
background information, it is perfectly intelligible to say that
the act of twiddling one's thumbs is morally good or morally
obligatory for its own sake. One is saying that it is correct to
disapprove of those who don't twiddle their thumbs and that
there is something amiss with our ordinary view that whether
or not one twiddles one's thumbs is a matter of indifference. It
is indeed true that we would fail to understand what a person
meant if he said that twiddling one's thumbs was a good action.
But the reason for this is not the one that Foot and Beardsmore
give. If I were to say that twiddling one's thumbs is a good action,
you would be confused and not know whether or not I was
claiming it to be an intrinsically good action. You would be
inclined to suspect that I was claiming it to be good in virtue
of some unrecognized characteristic such as its healthfulness
or its pleasingness to God; or, you might suspect that I did not

know the meaning of the word 'good'. But once you had assured yourself that I knew the meaning of the word 'good' (my saying that thumb-twiddling is a good action would not disqualify me as someone who knows the meaning of the word) and that I was claiming that twiddling one's thumbs is intrinsically good, you would understand me perfectly well.

In our conceptual scheme it is possible to assert the rightness or wrongness of *any action* and the goodness or badness of *anything*. This could not be the case if Foot's view were correct. Hare puts this point very well in the following passage:

That the descriptive meaning of the word 'good' is in morals, as elsewhere, secondary to the evaluative, may be seen in the following example. Let us suppose that a missionary, armed with a grammar book, lands on a cannibal island. The vocabulary of his grammar book gives him the equivalent, in the cannibals' language, of the English word 'good'. Let us suppose that, by a queer coincidence, the word is 'good'. And let us suppose, also, that it really is the equivalent – that it is, as the *Oxford English Dictionary* puts it, 'the most general adjective of commendation in their language.' If the missonary has mastered his vocabulary, he can, *so long as he uses the word evaluatively and not descriptively*, communicate with them about morals quite happily. They know that when he uses the word he is commending the person or object that he applies it to. The only thing they will find odd is that he applies it to such unexpected people, people who are meek and gentle and do not collect large quantities of scalps; whereas they themselves are accustomed to commend people who are bold and burly and collect more scalps than the average. But they and the missionary are under no misapprehension about the meaning, in the evaluative sense, of the word 'good'; it is the word one uses for commending. If they were under such a misapprehension, moral communication between them would be impossible.
We thus have a situation which would appear paradoxical to someone who thought that 'good' (either in English or in the cannibals' language) was a quality-word like 'red'. Even if the qualities in people which the missionary commended had nothing in common with the qualities which the cannibals commended, yet they would both know what the word 'good' meant. If 'good' were like 'red', this would be impossible; for then the cannibals' word and the English word would not be synonymous. If this were so, then when the missionary said that people who collected no scalps were good (English), and the cannibals said that people who collected a lot of scalps were good

(cannibal), they would not be disagreeing, because in English (at any rate missionary English), 'good' would mean, among other things, 'doing no murder', whereas in the cannibals' language 'good' would mean something quite different, among other things 'productive of maximum scalps'. It is because in its primary evaluative meaning 'good' means neither of these things, but is in both languages the most general adjective of commendation, that the missionary can use it to teach the cannibals Christian morals.[38]

Foot claims that we can sometimes draw evaluative conclusions from factual assumptions. For example, facts about how a person acts may commit us to saying that he is rude or courageous.[39] However, no amount of conceptual investigation can justify attitudes. If I do not share the favorable attitudes incorporated in our ordinary notion of courage I will simply refrain from using the word 'courage'. Similarly, the fact that the word 'nigger' has both descriptive and evaluative meaning does not commit anyone to holding black people in contempt. Those who don't have contempt for blacks can simply refrain from using the word 'nigger'.[40] Suppose that the term 'good action' meant what Foot claims it does, i.e., suppose that we can call an action good only if it either fulfills a special obligation or exemplifies a virtue. Suppose also that there is someone who claims that twiddling one's thumbs is an intrinsically good action and who views those who fail to do so with great disfavor. According to Foot, this person is simply mistaken in thinking that twiddling one's thumbs is an intrinsically good action. But this is at most a verbal point. Foot has no grounds on which to claim that the person's attitudes and prescriptions with respect to twiddling one's thumbs are in any way incorrect or erroneous. The thumb twiddler only needs to coin a new evaluative concept in terms of which to express himself.

*1.3.6. Reflection on the Question of What Would Constitute
        an Adequate Answer to Moral Skepticism Supports the
        Brentanist Theory*

Let me conclude this section of the chapter by generalizing on
an argument that was presented earlier. The argument is that no
attempt to give a rational justification for moral judgments could
be considered even minimally satisfactory or constitute any kind
of answer to moral skepticism unless it could show that certain
kinds of attitudes are correct or appropriate. This shows that *at
least part* of what is involved in making a moral judgment about
something is asserting that it is correct for people to have certain
attitudes about it. (Statements about the correctness of attitudes
constitute *necessary* conditions for the truth of moral judgments.
As we shall see in Chapter Two, this is all that is needed in order
to establish significant conclusions about the ideal observer
theory.) Suppose that a nihilist is completely indifferent to the
fact that he is doing things that bring pain and death to large
numbers of people. We may persuade him to accept a view according to which what he does is morally wrong and thus cause
him to accept judgments of the sort 'what I am doing is morally
wrong'. But unless he comes to concede that there is something
unsuitable about his attitudes and that his conduct is worthy of
disapprobation we would doubt that we had justified our views
to him, and doubt that he even thought that what he did was
morally wrong in our ordinary sense of the term. At the very
least, to think that something is wrong is to say that it merits
disapprobation. Strictly speaking, this argument does not establish the Brentanist Theory. It is, for example, compatible with
the view that moral judgments both: (a) have "descriptive meaning" in Foot's sense and (b) involve claims about the correctness
of attitudes. But we can make a strong case for the Brentanist
Theory by taking this argument together with our earlier criti-

cisms of Foot's view that moral terms have a fixed descriptive meaning.

1.3.7. Conclusion of Sections 1.2 and 1.3

Standard non-cognitivist theories cannot satisfactorily explain such things as moral disagreement, moral change and amoralism and immoralism; nor can they adequately account for the objectivity that moral judgments purport to have. The standard cognitivist theories do not give a satisfactory explanation of the practical and emotive force of moral judgments. The Brentanist Theory combines the virtues of each of these kinds of views. It accounts for both the purported objectivity and the practical import of morality. Brentano claims that his theory is able to reconcile the crucial role of feelings and emotions in moral judgments with the fact that they are objectively correct or valid for all rational beings.[41]

1.4. ANSWERS TO SOME OBJECTIONS TO THE BRENTANIST THEORY

1.4.1. Can the Brentanist Theory Provide a Satisfactory Account of the Difference Between Moral and Non-Moral Judgments?

One might object to the Brentanist Theory on the grounds that it cannot adequately account for the distinction between moral and aesthetic judgments. For some aesthetic judgments seem to involve claims about the correctness of attitudes. Consider the following:

(1)   My thinking that Lincoln was a good man.
(2)   My thinking that it was wrong for the Belgians to kill 15 million people in the Congo.

(3)   My thinking that Wagner was a better composer than
        Chopin.
(4)   My liking chocolate chip ice cream better than vanilla.
(5)   My thinking that Bonnie and Clyde were good bank
        robbers.

(5) is easily distinguishable from (1)–(4) in that it does not assert
the existence or the correctness of any attitudes about Bonnie and
Clyde. (5) simply describes Bonnie and Clyde with respect to a
certain function. I can be sincere in saying that they were good
bank robbers regardless of what attitude I have about them and
regardless of what attitude I believe it to be correct to have about
them. (4) differs from (1)–(3) in that it does not involve the
assertion of the correctness of any attitudes or preferences. When
I say that I like chocolate chip better than vanilla, I do not presume that it would be incorrect for others to like vanilla better,
or even that it would be incorrect for me to like vanilla better. Perhaps a gourmet who tells me that the food at the Waldorf is better
than the food at Burger King is asserting the correctness of certain
kinds of attitudes. But, for our purposes, this kind of judgment
can be treated in the same way as aesthetic judgments.

At least some aesthetic judgments are similar to moral judgments in that they involve the assertion of the correctness of
certain attitudes. Perhaps it would be preferable to phrase this as
follows: *some people* intend their aesthetic judgments to imply
the correctness of certain attitudes. For example, a man who says
that Wagner is better than Lawrence Welk may take this to imply
that it is correct to prefer listening to Wagner to listening to
Lawrence Welk. The Brentanist Theory does not, itself, explain
the difference between moral and aesthetic judgments. But this
difference can be accounted for within the context of the theory.
Part of the difference between moral and aesthetic judgments
lies in the kinds of attitudes and emotions that they assert to be

correct or incorrect. Unlike aesthetic judgments, moral judgments involve the assertion of the correctness of emotions such as guilt and remorse. To say that someone ought to do something is to imply, among other things, that it would be correct for him to feel guilt or remorse for failing to do it. I don't think that guilt can be distinguished from shame or mere displeasure with oneself on phenomenological grounds — it doesn't feel any different from shame or displeasure. What is distinctive about guilt is that it involves the belief that one is worthy of disapprobation or even punishment. Judgments of moral worth imply statements about the correctness of attitudes or preferences concerning the well-being of other people. To say that x is a more praise*worthy* person than y is to imply that, other things being equal, it is correct to prefer x's welfare to y's welfare. But this is not enough to distinguish all varieties of moral judgments from aesthetic judgments. We still have no way to distinguish between 'courage is good' (where 'good' is used in the sense of 'intrinsically good' rather than 'praiseworthy'), 'the Nietzschean *Übermensch* is a better sort of person than the Christian ideal', and 'Parsival is a great opera'. However, it is a *virtue* of the Brentanist Theory that it implies that certain kinds of moral judgments are not clearly distinguishable from aesthetic judgments. I take it as a partial confirmation for the Brentanist Theory that it implies that a normative theory such as Nietzsche's which is stripped of the distinctively moral notions of guilt, moral worth, and desert is not clearly distinguishable from an aesthetic theory. Nietzsche would not shrink from this conclusion.[42]

1.4.2. Can the Brentanist Theory Distinguish Between the Good and the Right, and the Bad and the Wrong?

A second objection to the Brentanist Theory is that it is so crude as to be unable to make any kind of distinction between different kinds of favorable and unfavorable moral judgments. The Brentanist Theory does not analyze the difference between calling something good and calling it right (or between calling something bad and calling it wrong) in terms of the correctness of different kinds of favorable and unfavorable attitudes. For example, we do not say that calling something good means that it is correct for everyone to have a favorable attitude (of type 1) about it and calling something right means that it is correct for everyone to have a favorable attitude (of type 2) about it. Any such view would be highly implausible on phenomenological grounds. It might seem that the Brentanist Theory can offer no satisfactory explanation of the difference between the right and the good and the wrong and the bad. I believe that this criticism is unfounded and will attempt to show how it is possible to distinguish between these notions within the context of the Brentanist Theory.

Consider the following case. S performs act x that promotes the general welfare and I have a favorable reaction to this action. What kind of (favorable) moral judgment does this reaction support? Does it support the claim that S is a good person, the claim that x is right, or the claim that x has good consequences? In order to answer this question we need to consider various hypothetical cases. When I say that S ought to do x I am saying that it is correct (for everyone) to choose or prefer that he do x rather than not, all other things being equal. When I say that it is wrong for him for do x I am saying that it would be correct (for everyone) to choose or prefer that he not do x. When I say that something is permissible but not obligatory I am saying that one could prefer either its performance or non-performance without being mistaken. It might be objected that in certain cases it could be correct to prefer that a certain act be performed, even if it is not obligatory. For example, it might be correct for everyone to prefer that S perform a noble act of supererogation rather than not. However, 'everyone' includes S and to say that it would be incorrect for him to prefer that he not perform the act of supererogation seems to be inconsistent with saying that it would be permissible for him not to do the act. I propose the following definition of supererogation:

> S's doing x is supererogatory if and only if: (1) It is not incorrect to prefer that he do x, (2) it is not incorrect to prefer that he not do x, and (3) S's doing x is praiseworthy and his not doing it is not blameworthy.

The goodness of the consequences of an action is determined by the kinds of attitudes that it would be correct to have about the consequences considered in isolation from all considerations of how they came about. For example, we can analyze the claim that S did his duty by not punishing an innocent person, even though doing so would have had better consequences, as follows:

(1)   It is correct to prefer S's not punishing the person to S's punishing him.

(2)   The results of his punishing the innocent person would be preferable to those of his not punishing him.

(2) requires considerable elaboration. Consider the following two possible universes:

(a)   The universe as it would be at t_1 if S punished the innocent person at t.

(b)   The universe as it would be at t_1 if S did not punish the innocent person at t.

To say that the consequences of S's punishing the innocent person would be better than those of his not punishing him is to say that if one of these two universes were to come into existence uncaused it would be correct to prefer or choose that it be (a) rather than (b). To this it might be objected that the idea of choosing that something occur uncaused is incoherent – if one chooses that something occur then its occurrence cannot be uncaused. I suggest either of the following replies to this objection. (i) The better state of affairs is the one that it would be correct to choose, if *per impossible*, one's causal efficacy in choosing it could be magically cancelled out and it would occur uncaused, or (ii) one state of affairs or situation is better than another if it would be correct to be pleased about it occurring uncaused (or by chance) *rather* than the other occurring uncaused (or by chance).

Many take the standard common sense objections to utilitarianism to be objections to any teleological theory of right and wrong. Teleological theories can be modified in order to minimize their counter-intuitiveness. For example, a teleologist who thinks that his theory is too permissive about such issues as lying and breaking promises might modify his theory of value so as to attribute great intrinsic disvalue to acts of lying and promise breaking. This would permit him to say that it would be wrong to lie or break promises, even in certain cases in which doing so would best promote the general welfare. It is possible to construct such a modified teleological theory of right and wrong that would be extensionally equivalent to the sort of deontological theory defended by Ross. Only those deontological theories that place absolute prohibitions on certain kinds of actions are clearly distinguishable from the kind of modified teleological theory under consideration. No matter how great a disvalue a teleologist attaches to such actions as deliberately punishing an innocent man his theory cannot yield an absolute prohibition against those actions. For performing such an act oneself may be necessary in order to prevent other occurrences of the same act. For example, my punishing one innocent man might be necessary in order to prevent the overthrow of a government that would be succeeded by one that would punish many more innocent people. I know of no way to distinguish between the statements 'lying is very bad' and 'lying is *prima facie* wrong' within the context of the sort of modified teleological theory under consideration here. This is not a serious problem, however, since there is no reason to suppose that we ought to be able to make such distinctions. I can only distinguish judgments about the rightness or wrongness of actions from judgments about the goodness or badness of their *causal consequences* (the intrinsic nature of the act is not a part of its own consequences). In (a) and (b), above, the act, itself, apart from any of its causal consequences, is specifically excluded from consideration.

I have suggested how to make out the difference between judgments of moral worth and other kinds of moral judgments earlier in this chapter (Section 1.1.2) and will not discuss this problem here.

1.4.3. Would It Be an Objection to the Brentanist Theory if Attitudes Cannot Be Objectively Correct?

One might object to the Brentanist Theory on the grounds that attitudes are not objectively correct, i.e., correct for all rational beings, in the way that Brentano claims. In the next chapter, I will argue that attitudes about moral questions are, at most, correct in the sense of being correct for all human beings. Here, I would like to argue that this and any other conceivable findings that might tend to undermine belief in the objectivity of morality are perfectly consistent with the claim that the Brentanist Theory is the correct account of the meaning of ordinary moral concepts. Brentano thinks that attitudes can be objectively correct or correct for all possible rational beings. Presumably, he takes moral judgments to involve the assertion of the objective correctness (as opposed to some weaker kind of correctness) of attitudes. Here, I am reluctant to follow Brentano. As we saw earlier in this chapter (Section 1.2.10) moral judgments do involve the implicit assertion that they are correct for all *human beings*. But it is not clear that moral judgments assert the correctness of certain attitudes for *all conceivable rational beings*. For instance, when I say that murder is wrong it is not certain that I am saying that it is correct for Martians and all other conceivable rational creatures to have an unfavorable attitude about murder. Such considerations are very remote from our ordinary thinking about moral questions. Since almost no one has ever even asked, much less answered, the question 'could it be correct for an extraterrestrial creature to approve of the killing of innocent human beings?', it seems clear that no answer to such a question can be said to be presupposed in our ordinary moral judgments and moral concepts.

But to allow this objection full force let us suppose that the Brentanist Theory should be taken to be the view that moral judgments are statements about the *objective* correctness of attitudes (this is *not* my view), and that attitudes cannot be objectively correct, or correct even in the weaker sense of being correct for all human beings. This still would not constitute an objection to the Brentanist Theory as a theory about what we *mean* when we make moral judgments. It would only commit us to an extreme version of what Mackie calls the "error theory", i.e., the view that all moral judgments are false or mistaken in virtue of purporting to be true or correct in some stronger sense than they actually are.[43] My own position, which will be developed more fully in the next chapter, commits me to a less extreme version of the error theory. I claim that any kind of moral judgment involves the assertion of the correctness of certain attitudes for all human beings and that there are many moral issues concerning which there is no attitude which is correct for all human beings.

CHAPTER TWO

THE IDEAL OBSERVER THEORY AND MORAL OBJECTIVISM

2.1. AN ARGUMENT FOR ACCEPTING THE IDEAL OBSERVER THEORY AS A STANDARD FOR DETERMINING THE CORRECTNESS OF MORAL JUDGMENTS

In this chapter I shall argue that there are no moral facts in the sense of 'moral fact' allowed by the Brentanist Theory. Then, I shall argue that this conclusion taken together with the Brentanist Theory entails that the Ideal Observer Theory (IOT) is the appropriate standard for determining the truth or correctness of moral judgments.

2.1.1. There Do Not Seem to Be Any Moral Facts in the Sense Allowed by the Brentanist Theory

Common sense holds that there are objective facts or truths about the external world. For example, it is a fact that the Earth is a greater distance from the Sun than is the planet Venus and that I am not now in pain. Among other things, this means that any rational being would be mistaken if he were to claim that Venus is farther from the Sun than the Earth or that I am now in pain. In order for there to be moral facts in this sense, there would have to be features of the world in virtue of which certain moral judgments are true or correct for all rational beings. For example, if it is a fact that accepting bribes is morally wrong, then it must be correct (in a sense that is opposed to incorrect) for any rational being to think that taking bribes is wrong.

43

Given the truth of the Brentanist Theory, a moral fact would have to be a feature of the world in virtue of which it is correct for all possible rational beings to have a certain sort of attitude about something. If it is a fact that accepting bribes is wrong, then it must be the case that it would be correct (in a sense that is opposed to mistaken) for any possible rational being to have an unfavorable attitude about accepting bribes, independently of the attitudes or beliefs that rational beings could or would have about bribery.

The strongest reason for rejecting moral realism is the implausibility of the theories that attempt to give an account of the nature of moral facts. There are two kinds of realist theories that are compatible with the Brentanist Theory. (1) Some realists hold that there being a moral fact about something consists in its being the case that it possesses some non-relational (natural or non-natural) property. For example, the fact that x is good consists in its being the case that x has the non-relational property of goodness. The non-relational property of goodness must be such that x's having it makes it correct (in a sense that is opposed to mistaken) for all possible rational beings to have a favorable attitude about x. (2) Other realists hold that moral facts consist in relations of "fittingness" or "appropriateness" holding between objects and particular sorts of attitudes about them.[1] (A variant of this is the view that the rightness or wrongness of an action consists in its fittingness or unfittingness in a particular sort of situation.) The first kind of view, which includes both naturalism and intuitionism, has, I believe, been thoroughly discredited. Most importantly, as I have already argued, such a view fails to explain the fact that moral considerations are supposed to provide us with reasons for action.

I shall not consider this position any further, but rather focus our attention on the claim that there are moral facts that consist in relations of fittingness holding between the things about which we make our moral judgments and particular sorts of attitudes about those things. The ideal observer theory also gives a theory about the fittingness or correctness of attitudes. According to the ideal observer theory, an attitude is correct or fitting if it would be shared by all who are fully informed and impartial, etc. Moral realism holds that attitudes can be correct for all possible rational beings, independently of what they believe or could believe. Therefore, for the realist, the correctness of an attitude must consist, not in its being acceptable to those who possess full information etc., but rather in some relation holding between the attitude and the object itself. According to the realist, the correctness of an attitude cannot be dependent on any contingent features of rational beings. Those who defend moral realism by appeal to this view (Ewing and Brentano), hold that the relation of fittingness is unanalyzable and self-evident to intuition. To this I can only reply that I fail to detect the existence of such relations. I find in their place strongly held convictions to the effect that certain attitudes are correct. The appeal to intuition and self-evidence is notoriously problematic in moral contexts because it is common for people to claim the truth of conflicting views on the basis of self-evidence. In the absence of any criteria for distinguishing between true and merely apparent self-evidence, we have reason to question the existence of the former. The ideal observer theory itself could be proposed as a criterion to distinguish between correct and incorrect intuitions. However, there does not seem to be any other plausible theory for distinguishing between correct and incorrect intuitions, and I conclude that moral realism is most likely false.

Not only are there reasons to question the existence of relations of fittingness holding directly between objects and particular sorts of attitudes about them, it is difficult to *conceive* of what such a relationship could *consist in*. Those philosophers who assert the existence of such relations (Ewing and Brentano) give no account of their nature. Ewing and Brentano do not even *attempt* to explain (much less succeed in explaining) how attitudes can "fit" objects or what this relation could consist in. For example, in virtue of what is it correct or fitting for every rational being to be displeased by the suffering of the virtuous? To assert the existence of moral facts or an objective moral order is not to explain *how* attitudes can be correct for all rational beings, it is only to assert that they somehow *are* objectively correct. A moral fact is a something, we know not what, that makes certain attitudes objectively correct. An obvious reply here is that, because fittingness *just is* a simple, unanalyzable relation, it is unreasonable to demand an account of its nature. But, this still leaves the notion of fittingness shrouded in mystery and does nothing to remove our doubts about the existence of this relation.

My own inability to conceive of how attitudes could be correct for all rational beings does not suffice to show that attitudes can't be objectively correct or that they, in fact, are not. Perhaps certain attitudes are objectively correct (correct for all rational beings) in some way that I have failed to conceive of. However, this kind of consideration cuts both ways. Since we cannot even begin to conceive of all of the different kinds of possible rational creatures, we can't be certain that any attitudes are correct for all of them. It is a commonplace that an attitude about something that is appropriate for one person to have may be inappropriate for a different sort of person or someone who stands in a different sort of relation to the thing in question. For example, it may be appropriate for a husband or wife to feel jealousy or resentment on account of a flirtatious spouse, but it is not appropriate for anyone else to feel jealous. It may be appropriate for a small child to be afraid of a playground bully, but it would not be appropriate for a prize fighter to be afraid of the bully. How much more would we expect there to be a great variation in the kinds of attitudes that are appropriate for radically different kinds of creatures. The point of all of this is not to show conclusively that there are no moral facts, but simply to make plausible the claim that there are none — that, itself, is enough to justify serious attention to the consequences that would follow if there were no moral facts.

2.1.2. Together, the Brentanist Theory and the (Apparent) Fact that There Are No Moral Facts Commit Us to a Version of the Ideal Observer Theory

Even if there are no moral facts in virtue of which attitudes can be said to be correct for all rational beings, we can still say that attitudes are correct or incorrect in virtue of their being dependent or non-dependent on one's having false beliefs or incomplete information, etc. For example, a person's hatred for the Jews is incorrect if it is dependent on his believing that Jewish treachery was responsible for the defeat of Germany in World War I. My favorable attitudes about Abraham Lincoln are correct, assuming that they would persist in the light of full knowledge about details of his life. There are no facts about the world independent of any relationship to the beliefs and attitudes of rational appraisers in virtue of which attitudes can be said to be either correct or incorrect. An attitude about something is correct provided that one could continue to hold it if one were fully informed and fully rational, etc. This amounts to saying that the correctness of attitudes must be determined by reference to some kind of conception of an ideal observer, and, given the Brentanist Theory, this is tantamount to saying that the IOT is the appropriate standard for determining the correctness of moral judgments.

On the weaker assumption that statements about the correctness of attitudes constitute only part of the meaning of moral judgments (see Note 6, Chapter One), our argument would show that the IOT provides necessary, but not sufficient, conditions for the truth of moral judgments. Suppose, for example, that 'x is good' entails 'it is correct to have a favorable attitude about x and incorrect to have any other kind of attitude about it'. Given this, we are entitled to conclude that *a necessary condition* of its being objectively true that x is good is that all ideal observers would have a favorable attitude about x.

Before proceeding to discuss the IOT, I should first note, however, that if my two assumptions (that the Brentanist Theory is true and that there are no moral facts) are mistaken, then it is doubtful that the IOT provides an appropriate standard for assessing the correctness of moral judgments. The IOT defines 'the correct view' as 'the view that people would accept under ideal conditions'. If we reject the IOT and say that the correctness of moral judgments is determined by independently existing moral facts, then there is no longer any reason to suppose that we are constituted so as to arrive at the correct views under ideal conditions. As a limiting case, we can conceive of the possibility that we were created in such a way as to make judgments contrary to the moral facts even under the most ideal conditions. Therefore, even though philosophers are wont to postulate the existence of 'moral facts' in order to account for our alleged knowledge about moral questions, the belief in objective moral facts undermines our claims to moral knowledge. Moral facts are sufficiently mysterious that, if there are any, it is possible that our own views are greatly at variance with them.[2]

2.2. FIRTH'S VERSION OF THE IDEAL OBSERVER THEORY

Roderick Firth's paper 'Ethical Absolutism and the Ideal Observer' is the classic statement of the IOT in contemporary moral philosophy. In this section of the chapter I shall present Firth's theory and then argue that, contrary to what Firth says, his theory fails to support even the most modest version of objectivism.

2.2.1. Firth's Theory

Firth analyzes the meaning of moral concepts in terms of the notion of an ideal observer. According to Firth, moral judgments of the sort 'x is ____' (where '____' is a moral predicate such as 'good' or 'bad' or 'right' or 'wrong') are to be analyzed along the following lines: 'all ideal observers would react in such and such ways to x'. Very roughly, to make a favorable moral judgment about something, to say that it is good or right etc., is to say that all ideal observers would feel moral approval for it. To make an unfavorable moral judgment about something is to say that all ideal observers would feel moral disapproval for it. Moral approval and disapproval are felt desires or aversions that are characterized by a "demand quality".[3] Moral approval or disapproval cannot be defined as certain kinds of feelings that are produced by one's moral beliefs. For that would make Firth's analysis of moral terms viciously circular. It would be circular to say that 'x is a right action' means that 'all idea observers would believe that x is right and, as a result, have such and such kind of favorable emotion concerning it'.[4]

The characteristics that Firth takes to be essential for being an ideal observer are the following: (1) he is omniscient with respect to all non-moral facts, (2) he is omnipercipient, i.e., he is able to imagine vividly any possible events or states of affairs, including the experiences and subjective states of other people, (3) he is disinterested, that is, he has no interests or desires that involve essential reference to any particular individuals or things; all of his interests are general (for example, an ideal observer cannot desire that Smith be happy or that the Cathedral of Ulm be preserved for their own sake; he can, however, desire that all humans be happy or that all beautiful buildings be preserved and desire these things for their own sake), (4) he is dispassionate, i.e., he has no emotions that are directed upon objects because they are believed to have essentially particular features, for example, an ideal observer cannot love someone because it is *his* child or *his* parent, (5) he is consistent, and (6) he is a *"normal"* human being.[5]

2.2.2. Firth's Theory Contrasted with Brandt's Version of the IOT

It would be useful to contrast Firth's theory with the version of the ideal observer theory formulated by Richard Brandt in Chapter 10 of *Ethical Theory*. Unlike Firth, Brandt does not use the notion of an ideal observer to provide an analysis of the meaning of moral terms. He only uses it to provide a standard for the correctness of moral judgments.[6] The second major difference between Firth's theory and Brandt's is that Brandt holds that the correctness of a moral judgment is determined by whether or not an ideal observer would accept it, and not, as Firth claims, by the attitudes that ideal observers would have concerning the subject of the judgment. According to Brandt, a moral judgment is true or correct if and only if it would be accepted by someone who was (1) impartial, (2) fully informed, and (3) in a "normal" state of mind, and (4) such that the attitude that his judgment expresses is compatible with his having a system of principles that is both consistent and general.[7] The criticisms that I will make of Firth's theory apply equally to Brandt's theory and the revisions of Firth's theory that I shall suggest later are also applicable to Brandt's theory.

2.2.3. *Ideal Observers Might Disagree in Their Views or Attitudes About Certain Moral Issues; Therefore, Firth's Theory Fails to Support a Strong Version of Moral Objectivism*

In order for Firth's theory to support a strong objectivist view, it is necessary that all ideal observers would have the same attitudes about all conceivable moral questions. If there are only some moral issues concerning which all ideal observers would have the same attitudes, then the ideal observer theory supports an intermediate view between extreme objectivism and extreme meta-ethical relativism. According to this intermediate view, there is an objectively correct view or judgment concerning *some*, but not all, moral questions. If there are no moral issues about which all ideal observers would have the same attitudes, then the IOT supports an extreme version of meta-ethical relativism according to which there are no moral issues concerning which there is an objectively correct view.[8]

In order to show that Firth's theory fails to support the strong version of ethical objectivism, it is only necessary to find a single moral issue about which it would be possible for different ideal observers to have conflicting attitudes. Such issues are not difficult to find. Consider some of the questions concerning the morality of lying. Is it permissible for a doctor to lie to a patient about the patient's medical condition if he thinks that it is likely that the patient will die of fright if he learns of the seriousness of his condition? Firth gives no reasons to suppose that ideal observers could not have incompatible attitudes about such questions. Moreover, it seems reasonably certain that they could. For the essential characteristics of an ideal observer are not sufficient to (causally) determine his attitudes about such questions. People's attitudes about such things as lying depend, in large measure, on their background and moral training. Given appropriate differences in background and moral training, it is quite possible that there are issues about which two ideal observers could have conflicting attitudes that were characterized by a demand quality. Firth's theory does nothing to rule out the possibility that different ideal observers could have received radically different kinds of moral training.

2.2.4. Duncker's Attempt to Show that All Disagreements About Moral Questions Are Dependent on Disagreements About Matters of Fact

There are no doubt some who would reject this and contend that human beings are so constituted that it is psychologically impossible for them to hold conflicting views or attitudes about something if they share the same empirical or factual beliefs about it. The most noteworthy defense of this position that I am familiar with is Karl Duncker's paper 'Ethical relativity'.[9] Duncker considers a number of instances in which different societies hold incompatible views about the moral status of a certain kind of action. He contends that in all such cases the action has different "situational meanings" in different cultural settings. Therefore, these cases do not constitute instances of disagreement about the moral status of a certain kind of action, but rather cases in which different evaluations are given of similar, but ultimately different, kinds of actions (at least the actions are believed to be different in kind). He cites usury as an example. In previous times the taking of interest on money lent was generally frowned upon, but today it is thought to be permissible.

But do we in both cases deal with the *same* act? Is money always identical with money, or interest with interest? From a genetical [sic] point of view the usage of the identical word is justified. But in the early stages of civilization loans were employed predominantly for consumption, whereas in capitalism loans are employed mainly as capital for profitable production. That makes all the difference. Where the borrower borrows in order to gain, it is only fair to make the lender a partner in the undertaking by paying him some "share in the profit." Interest no longer means an exploitation of necessities or passions. It has changed its typical "meaning."[10]

Duncker fails to mention or account for the fact that much of the money borrowed in our society is used for consumption — home mortgages, automobile loans, and credit for smaller household items. He does not show any relevant difference between this and the kind of lending that aroused so much disapproval during the Middle Ages.

Duncker's treatment of certain other examples is even less plausible. He claims that the view that an individual is an organic component of society just as an arm or a leg is a part of a body underlies certain moral perspectives that are opposed to our own.

Where the individual is felt to be a mere "limb of the group body" we should be the less surprised at the body's decision to sacrifice one of its limbs.

This meaning of a man as a "limb" rather than a "person of his own" is extremely important for a genuine *ethical* understanding of many other phenomena. For instance, blood-revenge is not genuinely understood unless one takes into consideration that the victim is felt to be just an organ, the available "vulnerable spot" of the other clan, which as a collective whole, is felt to be the real offender.[11]

However, to view an individual as a part of an organism is not to entertain any factual or empirical beliefs concerning him. It is rather to hold a certain sort of attitude about him. This attitude constitutes an ultimate moral perspective. Duncker's arguments fail to show that the opposed moral perspectives of different communities rest entirely on differences in belief. His thesis becomes even less plausible when one considers disagreements between particular individuals. I think that everyone who has discussed moral issues seriously with other people has encountered conflicts of opinion that persist in the light of apparent agreement about factual matters and which further factual inquiry does not seem capable of resolving. I once became involved in a serious dispute with my father concerning the question of whether we should inform my grandmother of a pulmonary embolism reported to us by her physician. We both agreed that this knowledge would cause her considerable distress and that there was some chance that it would worsen her condition or even lead to her death. My father maintained that this information should be concealed from her. I strongly believed that her right to know and perpare herself for death overrode the utilitarian considerations to which my father appealed. We were unable to discover any significant factual disagreements between us. Of course, it is unlikely, and in any case impossible to be sure, that we shared all of the same beliefs in this instance. However, it is virtually certain that such cases reveal ultimate moral disagreements. For it is easy to imagine various possible descriptions of the relevant facts which are such that if we each accepted those descriptions we would continue to disagree. I believe, for instance, that my father and I would have continued to disagree about what ought to be done if we had both agreed that she would live for 2 more years with the knowledge and 3 more years without it.

2.2.5. Firth's Ideal Observers Would Not All Agree in Their Attitudes About Any Moral Questions; Therefore, Firth Is Committed to an Extreme Version of Relativism

Not only does Firth's theory fail to support ethical objectivism, there are reasons to think that it actually supports extreme relativism. I shall take views and attitudes about issues such as Nazism and genocide to be the test case for this. If there are any moral judgments that are objectively correct, it is likely to be such judgments as that it was wrong for the Nazis to have killed the Jews. (If ideal observers would not all share unfavorable attitudes about these deeds, then it is unlikely that they would agree in their attitudes about any moral moral issues.) The question that concerns us here is whether it is empirically possible for a human being who possesses the essential characteristics of an ideal observer to approve of the "final solution" and things of that ilk. I do not think that I can offer a definite answer to this question. However, what we know about the effectiveness of early moral training suggests that this is indeed possible. Attitudes and views that we learn as young children have a tendency to persist in the light of the strongest possible criticisms later in life. Given a sufficiently forceful and effective early indoctrination in Nazism, it is at least conceivable that a person could persist in those views and attitudes, even if he were to acquire all of the characteristics of an ideal moral observer. (Being an ideal observer and being aware of all the relevant facts would presumably involve the awareness of the falsity of many of the beliefs that were imparted to one as a part of one's indoctrination.)

The views and attitudes of Nazis and those of similar persuasion are frequently (perhaps characteristically) an outlet for free-floating anger and hostility aroused by other sources. Such views can be a source of emotional gratification for those who feel a kind of objectless rage. A person who has suffered great indignities and frustrations in life without being able to give adequate expression to his anger may obtain considerable relief from his frustration by venting his spleen against the Jews or other minority groups, even if the ultimate causes of his anger have little, if anything, to do with the activities of members of those groups. Firth's theory does not rule out the possibility that an ideal observer could have a great deal of free-floating anger and thus also a predilection towards views and attitudes that constitute an outlet for that anger.

The requirement that ideal observers be disinterested and dispassionate does nothing to rule out the possibility that an ideal observer might approve of Nazism. For attitudes or emotions about an entire group or class of people do not count as "particular interests" on his view.[12] It is possible to give a stronger reading to the disinterestedness of the ideal observer. Adopting Rawls's notion of impartiality, we could say that an ideal observer must be ignorant of his own personal situation in life. Among other things, this would mean that an ideal observer could not be aware of which ethnic group he is a member. Given this conception of impartiality, all ideal observers would have very strong self-interested reasons to disapprove of the slaughter of any group of people, because they would know that they might belong to that group. But not even this kind of impartiality insures that all ideal observers would disapprove of genocide. For sometimes hatred for others can be stronger than self-love. It is entirely possible that a person could be so thoroughly indoctrinated in anti-semitic attitudes that he would view the extermination of the Jews with favor, even if he thought that there was some possibility that he, himself, were Jewish.[13] The same arguments can be given to show that Brandt's theory fails to support even the most limited kind of objectivism.

2.3. MY CHARACTERIZATION OF THE IDEAL OBSERVER

2.3.1. An Ideal Observer Must Be Fully Informed

To the extent that a person's moral judgments are the result of his being mistaken or ignorant of certain relevant facts, they are also to that extent objectionable from a rational point of view. If there is a view that would be accepted only by people who were mistaken or ill-informed about certain relevant facts, then that view is in a fairly clear sense incorrect or mistaken. (Let me stress here that my claim is not that a view is mistaken because some or all of its proponents *are* ill-informed, but rather that a view is incorrect *if it could only be accepted by people who were ill-informed or who fell short of being ideal observers in other ways.*)

(a) *Some difficulties in formulating the requirement of full information*. There are serious difficulties in formulating the requirement that ideal observers must know all of the relevant facts. To say that a given fact is or is not relevant to a particular moral issue is to presuppose certain substantive normative views. The IOT cannot serve its intended purpose of justifying first-order normative views if it presupposes any such views in its formulation. Firth is aware of this problem and suggests that we conceive of the ideal observer as someone who is *omniscient* with respect to all non-moral facts. In that way we can be sure that the ideal observer is aware of all of the relevant facts without making any assumptions about which facts are relevant and which are not.[14] The trouble with this is that the ideal observer's omniscience is incompatible with his humanity. Human beings are not capable of knowing everything. It is not intelligible to ask how someone would react to various things if he were omniscient. It is like trying to determine how I would behave if I were an utterly different kind of person. Brandt suggests the following solution to this problem: the relevant facts that the ideal observer must know are all of the facts that would make a difference in his ethical reaction to a given case.[15]

Firth offers the following objection to Brandt's proposal:

there is no *one* body of facts (F) vivid awareness of which would make a difference to the manner in which an ideal observer[1] reacts to situation S. The body of facts would vary with the false beliefs of the ideal observer[1]. And for any fact, indeed, we could find *some* set of false beliefs which would make that fact seem to be ethically relevant to S.[16]

We could say instead that an ideal observer must know all of the facts about S that would make a difference in his reaction to it *if he had no false beliefs*. But as Firth also notes, there is still the problem that "the facts which would seem relevant to situation S at a given time, would depend to some extent on the number

and character of the ideal observer's *true* beliefs at that time."[17]
For example, suppose that x and y are betrothed to each other
and that y marries z. y's knowledge of the laws concerning breach
of promise is relevant to a moral assessment of this situation.
However, Brandt's criterion will not give the ideal observer knowledge of this unless he knows or believes that x and y were once
betrothed; unless he believes this his views about the extent of
y's knowledge of the laws concerning breach of contract will not
make a difference in his reactions. Firth's argument depends on
the fact that we cannot say unqualifiedly whether or not knowing
a particular fact would make a difference in a person's reaction
to something. For whether or not a particular belief would make
a difference depends on the person's other beliefs.

If we wish, therefore, to avoid excluding some particular fact which is ethically relevant to S, we must attribute to the ideal observer[1] enough true
beliefs to guarantee that his ethical reactions would be affected if he became
aware of this additional fact. In order to guarantee this by assigning some
general characteristic to the ideal observer[1], however, we should have to say
that the ideal observer[1] has true beliefs about *all other relevant facts*. And
this, of course, would involve us in a vicious circle, since there is no way to
define "relevant fact" except by reference to the very test which we are now
attempting to formulate. . . . And this means that we are brought back again
to the conclusion that an ideal observer must be omniscient with respect to
non-ethical facts.[18]

This problem can be avoided if we adopt the following principle:
a fact x is relevant to a judgment about y if and only if either
(1) knowing x would make a difference to an ideal observer's
reaction to y, or (2) x is a member of a group of facts G such that
knowing G would make a difference in an ideal observer's reactions to y, and there is no subset of G the knowledge of which
would have exactly the same effect on his reactions to y.[19]

(b) *Having full information requires a knowledge and vivid representation of the experiences of other people.* The requirement

of full information includes the full knowledge and understanding of the feelings of others — when that is relevant. For example, in order to be in a good position to make a judgment about the moral status of the decision of a head of state to begin a war, it is not enough to know how many people will be killed or wounded, it is necessary to know about the experiences of those who are affected by the war. One needs to know how it feels to be burned alive or blown to pieces, how it feels to have someone shooting at one, how it feels to not have a face, or to lose a limb or one's sexual organs, how it feels to have a loved one killed in the army, and so on. Lack of this kind of knowledge clearly constitutes ignorance of relevant considerations.[20]

In addition to being fully informed, an ideal observer must also 'adequately represent' those things or states of affairs about which he makes his judgments. It is not enough that he knows about them in some dispositional sense, he must have the things he knows vividly present before his mind. The person who knows certain relevant information, but who fails to picture it vividly, has ignored it or put it out of mind. 'Hardening one's heart' to the suffering of others typically consists in *refusing* to represent vividly their suffering to oneself, even though one may, in some dispositional sense, know what it is like. Not only is it morally objectionable to harden one's heart, doing so constitutes a cognitive failing in terms of which we can criticize one's views and attitudes.

(c) *Some ways in which the requirement that ideal observers must adequately represent other people's experiences helps to insure that they will agree in their attitudes*. Many cases of disagreement in attitude about moral questions can be accounted for in terms of a failure on the part of one or more of the parties to represent adequately the experiences of other people. I am convinced that the stances of jingoists and others who take a cavalier attitude about war are dependent on their failing to picture adequately or comprehend fully the horrors of war. The IOT can resolve such disagreements in a manner that supports moral objectivism. The following lines from Blake, which Hare quotes in a similar context, seem appropriate here:

> Can I see another's woe
> And not be in sorrow too?
> Can I see another's grief
> And not seek for kind relief?[21]

Here I would also like to note one other respect in which the requirement of full information can, by itself, insure a greater measure of agreement in the emotional reactions of ideal observers. A factor that accounts for many disagreements about moral questions is the relative instructiveness of people's life experiences. Consider the case of a person who has experienced great misfortunes on account of having been lied to at various times in his life. He is likely to endorse very strict principles against lying. On the other hand, a person who has suffered greatly because of other people's having refused to lie in order to protect him might be inclined to take a very permissive view about lying. We might be inclined to say that each person has overlearned a certain kind of lesson. The one has a vivid awareness of the bad consequences that can result from lying, the other has a vivid awareness of the bad consequences that can result from rigid adherence to rules forbidding lying. An ideal observer would have a vivid awareness of each. To the extent that disagreements about moral questions are the result of such limitations in our experiences, the IOT is capable of resolving them.

(d) *What is involved in 'adequately representing' another person's experiences?* We need to determine what is involved in adequately representing another person's experiences to oneself. Before attempting to do this, however, it would be helpful to consider some of the various ways of representing or understanding the experiences of others.

(i) *Emotional infection*. Emotional infection is a transference of feelings from one creature to another. Emotional infection most typically occurs in crowds or large groups. In such situations, an individual is likely to take on the mood of those around him. This is why people sometimes attempt to make themselves feel better by seeking out cheerful company or smiling faces. To be 'infected' by the emotions of others entails that one feels or undergoes those same emotions oneself. Emotional infection does not presuppose any knowledge or understanding of the feelings of others. The feelings that one undergoes are not necessarily represented as being shared by others. Emotional infection can occur in groups of animals or infants who have no knowledge or understanding of the fact that their experiences are shared by others.[22]

(ii) *Sympathy*. In order for one to be said to sympathize with another person's feelings it is necessary that one know or understand what it is like to experience them. But this is not sufficient for sympathy. At the very least, it is necessary that one have the other person's experiences present to mind. Suppose that I see someone smash his finger with a hammer. I know from my own experience what it feels like to do this, but unless I can call up a mental image of his pain I cannot be said to sympathize with him. We can represent the experiences of others to our imagination in just the same way that we can imagine or picture sights and sounds and smells, etc. Having a mental image of another person's experiences does not entail undergoing those same kinds of experiences oneself. And, contrary to what Hume, Smith, Schopenhauer, and Stein say, it is possible to sympathize with or have compassion for another person without undergoing those same experiences at the time oneself.[23] I can sympathize with a person who is having a headache without having a headache myself. Sympathy requires being moved emotionally by the other person's feelings. To sympathize with another person's suffering (of whatever sort) entails feeling distressed or saddened oneself.[24] If I am indifferent to another person's distress, I cannot be said to sympathize with him. Sympathy should not be considered an essential feature of the ideal observer; one need not sympathize with another person's feelings in order to represent them adequately. In sympathy the representation of another person's experiences is separable from one's emotional response to it. The IOT purports to give us standards for determining when attitudes about such things as human suffering are appropriate or inappropriate. It cannot serve this function if we make having certain kinds of attitudes about the experiences of others part of the definition of what it is to be an ideal observer. It may be the case that all human beings who adequately represent the feelings of others and who satisfy the other conditions for being ideal observers are sympathetic. But, if this is true, it is not true as a matter of definition but only as a matter of empirical fact.

(iii) *Emotional identification*. Sometimes we imagine ourselves in the position of others so well that we undergo roughly the same sorts of emotions that they are experiencing. Almost everyone is familiar with the phenomenon of feeling fright or anxiety or joy as a result of identifying with other people or fictional characters. The fear and anxiety of a crowd watching a man on a tightrope is an especially good example of this. The crowd will cringe and shake with fear as they imagine themselves in his place. Emotional identification can enable those who have reasonably good powers of imagination to undergo emotions that are very similar to those of the people with whom they are identifying. I can, for example, feel the grief and sorrow of the Joads as they leave Oklahoma when I read *The Grapes of Wrath*. Emotional identification cannot give us an adequate representation of the feelings of others if we simply imagine how *we* would feel in their situation. We must also imagine ourselves as having their hopes and desires and aversions, etc. While our powers of imagination and identification can give us a good knowledge of the *emotions* of other people, they do not generally provide us with any insight into the nature of the physical sensations that others experience. If I strongly identify with a person who I see being crushed to death in an accident, I can experience something like the terror and anguish that he feels, but I do not in any way experience the kind of physical pain that he suffers.[25]

Our understanding of the feelings of others is ultimately rooted in our knowledge of our own experiences. A person who has never felt emotional distress or physical pain cannot have an adequate understanding of human or animal suffering. With reasonably good powers of imagination one can understand the feelings of others in circumstances very different from one's own. I can understand the feelings of disappointment suffered by a politician upon losing an election even though I have never been in such a position myself. (This understanding is dependent on my own immediate acquaintance with feelings of disappointment and frustration.) Often our understanding of the feelings of others is hampered by limited powers of imagination or an unwillingness to use them. Limitations in our own personal experiences can also place bounds on our understanding of the feelings of others. A person who has never felt extreme physical pain cannot know what it feels like to be tortured or burned alive.[26]

(iv) *Is it necessary that one undergo similar experiences oneself?* To return to our question, what constitutes an adequate *representation* of another person's feelings, e.g., your sorrow at the death of a loved one? As we have seen, it is not sufficient that one understand or know what the experience is like in some dispositional sense. One must have the experience immediately and vividly to mind. Can a mental image of an experience be a fully adequate representation, or is it necessary that one undergo a qualitatively identical experience? I know of no *a priori* reasons for thinking that it would be impossible for a mental image to constitute an adequate representation of an experience. However, when I reflect on my own case, it seems evident to me that I am unable to form an adequate image of any of my own experiences. For example, the image of impending pain that I have in the dentist's waiting room is never a fully adequate representation of the pain that ensues. I take this to be at least some reason for thinking that having an adequate representation of one's own experiences or those of other people involves undergoing similar experiences oneself. I shall call the version of the IOT that requires that ideal observers directly undergo experiences of a kind similar to those that are involved in the moral issues upon which they reflect the 'direct experience version' of the IOT. The choice between the direct experience and non-direct experience versions of the IOT is a matter of considerable importance. For the direct experience version of the IOT is more likely to insure that all ideal observers will have the same views and attitudes about some things, and thus it seems capable of supporting a stronger version of moral objectivism than its rival. The direct experience version of the IOT implies that in order to represent another person's experiences adequately an ideal observer must undergo a similar kind of experience at the time himself. Suppose that an ideal observer represents another person's pain to himself. The ideal observer will presumably have an unfavorable attitude about the pain that *he* suffers in representing the other person's pain. This is not the same as his having a negative attitude about the other person's pain. However, the ideal observer's negative attitude about his own suffering is likely to be carried over to his attitudes about the sufferings of the other person. It is very unlikely that the IOT can support a strong version of objectivism unless all ideal observers would agree in having favorable attitudes about the pleasure and well being of others and unfavorable attitudes about their suffering. The direct experience version of the IOT seems much more likely to secure this kind of agreement than other versions of the IOT.

(e) *Is the ability to represent adequately the experiences of other people compatible with one's being human?* There would seem to be many cases in which it would be impossible for an ideal observer (who must, as I shall argue later, be a human being) to represent adequately all of the relevant facts. No one can even begin to picture all of the consequences of a war that may cause death and suffering to millions of people. This is a significant difficulty for the IOT. There are two ways of dealing with this problem — neither of which is entirely satisfactory. First, we could say that the correctness of moral judgments is determined by the attitudes that the ideal observer would have or the judgments that he would make *if he could adequately represent all of the relevant facts.* But it may not make any sense to talk about how someone would react if he could do something that he cannot do and could not do without becoming a very different sort of person. Alternatively, we could say that a (favorable or unfavorable) moral judgment about something is correct if and only if all ideal observers would have favorable or unfavorable attitudes about it if they represented the relevant facts as well as it is possible for them to do. This also seems unsatisfactory, since we can always suppose that the reactions of the ideal observer might have been different if he had been able to represent the relevant facts more adequately. It seems as if his actual judgments or emotional reactions are discredited if they are a consequence of limitations in his powers of representation.

(f) *Will an ideal observer be too squeamish in his reactions?* It might be argued that the ideal observer's vivid representation of relevant facts would cause him to be excessively emotional and squeamish in his judgments. To the extent that he vividly represents the relevant facts he will be unable to approve of courses of action having gruesome or unpleasant consequences. For example, it might be argued that an ideal observer could not approve of abortion or any acts of war if he had all of their gruesome details vividly present to mind. To this I simply reply that there could be no better argument for the immorality of war, abortion, or anything else than that we could not fail to disapprove of it in light of a full awareness of all of its consequences. However, it should be noted that mere squeamishness cannot determine the reactions of an ideal observer. An ideal observer who is repelled by the gruesomeness of abortion must also have it vividly to mind that equally gruesome things such as open-heart surgery are morally beyond reproach. The ideal observer who is repelled by the horrors brought about by the Allied forces during the Second World War would be even more repelled by the greater horrors that would have ensued if the Axis Powers had been victorious. (An ideal observer would approve of those actions which were *required* to achieve the victory of the Allies.) What is crucial to note here is that an aversion to certain gruesome aspects of something does not necessarily count as an (overall) unfavorable attitude for the purposes of our theory.

2.3.2. A Way of Strengthening Firth's Requirement that Ideal Observers Be Fully Informed

The requirement that ideal observers must be fully informed can be strengthened. Not only should we demand that an ideal observer be fully informed *at the time that he deliberates about moral questions*, we should also require that he not have accepted any false beliefs or have been ignorant of any relevant facts *at any time in the past when his attitudes were being formed*. The fact that a person's views or attitudes about something are dependent on his having been ignorant or mistaken about it in the past seems to be just as much a reason for discrediting them as the fact that they are dependent on his being ignorant or mistaken about it in the present. The reason why this additional requirement is necessary is that ignorance or false beliefs can continue to affect one's views and attitudes about moral questions even if they are corrected at some later time. Let us consider our test case of Nazism. The dissemination of false beliefs about the characteristics of Jews and other despised groups is an essential part of Nazi indoctrination. It is very doubtful that it could succeed unless those being indoctrinated adopted a number of such beliefs. The case of Nazi indoctrination raises considerable difficulties for standard versions of the IOT, for the attitudes of a person who has undergone such indoctrination are likely to persist, even if he becomes fully informed later on. The additional requirement about having been fully informed in the past enables us to deal more easily with this kind of case. We can discount the views and attitudes of a Nazi if they are dependent on his having held false beliefs in the past.

A more commonplace example of the persistence of attitudes based upon false beliefs even after those beliefs have been rejected has to do with attitudes concerning sexual morality. The views and attitudes of those who believe that homosexuality is a great moral evil are usually a result of (what I take to be) false beliefs such as that God disapproves of homosexuality and that he will subject homosexuals to eternal torture in the afterlife. It is very common for people to continue in those attitudes, even if they later come to reject the factual beliefs upon which they are founded.[27]

2.3.3. The Views and Attitudes of an Ideal Observer Cannot Be Dependent on His Having Been Influenced by Others Who Are Not Ideal Observers

We should also require that the attitudes of an ideal observer not be dependent on the direct or indirect influence of people who are ignorant of relevant information or who fall short of being ideal observers in other respects. An attitude is correct only if it could have arisen in a world in which all past and present people were ideal observers. The reason that some such condition is necessary is that there may be views and corresponding attitudes that could not arise in a world in which all people were ideal observers, but which an ideal observer could accept as a result of moral training or the influence of others. For example, if no one had ever held (what I take to be) mistaken beliefs to the effect that God abhors and punishes homosexuality and all forms of premarital sex, then it is unlikely that anyone could be horrified by all forms of homosexual and premarital sexual activity or view them as great moral evils. (Perhaps some individuals could find puritanical views and attitudes about sexual morality to be a gratifying way to displace hostility. But I shall ignore this difficulty here, since I will later give an argument for disqualifying anyone whose attitudes involve emotional displacement as an ideal observer.) However, even someone who never held any false beliefs about God's attitudes regarding sexuality and who did not fall short of being an ideal observer in any other respects could conceivably come to hold such attitudes if most or all of his associates held them. (The extent of human conformity argues in favor of this possibility.) The fact that an attitude could be adopted by someone who was fully informed and who had all of the other essential characteristics of an ideal observer does not show that the attitude is correct or rationally defensible. For his adopting it may still be dependent on his having been influenced by people who were ill-informed or fell short of being ideal observers in other respects. In order to be correct an attitude must be such that it could have arisen in a world in which all people were ideal observers.

2.3.4. An Ideal Observer Must Have Full Knowledge of All Relevant Moral Principles

As a corollary to the requirement of full information (knowledge of all the relevant empirical facts) we should also require that an ideal observer possess full knowledge of all of the possible moral principles that bear on the issues in question and a vivid awareness of the implications of all of those principles. It is also fair to require that an ideal observer have possessed this knowledge at all times in the past when his attitudes were being formed. An attitude about something is discredited if it is dependent on one's having been ignorant of principles or the consequences of principles that bear on the thing in question at times in the past when one's attitudes were being formed. This additional requirement strengthens the theory in a number of important respects. For disagreements between people about moral questions can often be accounted for by their ignorance of certain relevant principles or their ignorance of the implications of the principles that they consider. For example, it is not uncommon for people reflecting about the moral status of lying to suppose that the rejection of an absolute prohibition against lying constitutes an acceptance of the view that it is permissible to lie whenever one pleases. But this supposition rests on the mistaken assumption that 'lying is always wrong' and 'lying is always permissible' are the only possible general principles about the morality of lying. People often fail to realize all of the implications of the principles that they accept or consider. For instance, a person who says that it is always wrong to lie may not realize that this commits him to the view that it would be wrong to lie in order to save the life of an innocent person. To the extent that disagreements about moral questions result from people's ignorance of relevant principles or their ignorance of the implications of various principles (and just as important, to the extent that disagreement depends on one's attitudes having been formed at times in the past when one was ignorant of such things), our revised version of the IOT can resolve these disagreements. For an ideal observer is someone who is aware of all of the relevant principles and their implications.

2.3.5. The Attitudes and Judgments of an Ideal Observer Cannot Involve 'Emotional Displacement'

Negative moral judgments often involve emotional displacement. Unfavorable moral judgments about something often constitute an outlet for repressed or ungratified emotions aroused by other sources. For example, a man who is extremely angry with his employer but unable to avenge himself or even express his anger for fear of being fired may find some relief from his pent-up rage by coming to the view that the head of a hostile foreign power deserves to be killed in a painful manner. As is the case with other emotions, anger and hatred tend to become more intense if they are repressed. Repression also has a tendency to make emotions fester or be 'relived'. Scheler defines 'ressentiment' as a reliving or re-experiencing of hostile emotions such as hatred, envy, revenge and the like that is typically caused by an inability to act out such feelings (the inability to express hatred, the inability to take vengeance, and the inability to acquire the things for which one envies others).[28] The paradigm example of *ressentiment* is someone whose repressed hostility has festered so much that it ceases to have any definite objects. Such individuals derive gratification from any kind of unfavorable moral judgment.

The impulse to detract, however, is not in the same sense tied to definite objects — it does not arise through specific causes with which it disappears.

On the contrary, this affect *seeks* those objects, those aspects of men and things, from which it can draw gratification. It likes to disparage and to smash pedestals, to dwell on the negative aspects of excellent men and things. [29]

People who have a great deal of pent-up anger can obtain emotional gratification from holding the most appalling sorts of attitudes and moral judgments. Almost any kind of moral judgment (and corresponding attitude) can serve as a source of emotional gratification given appropriate circumstances. Thus, it seems unlikely that there could be sufficient agreement in the attitudes of ideal observers to insure that the IOT supports even the most minimal version of objectivism unless we can justify some kind of restriction concerning emotional displacement.

I shall now attempt to provide a justification for saying that the attitudes of ideal observers cannot involve any kind of emotional displacement. [30] According to the ideal observer theory, the correctness of a moral judgment about something is determined by the attitudes that *it* would arouse in someone under ideal circumstances — when he is fully informed, etc. If a moral judgment or attitude about something involves 'emotional displacement', then the thing in question did not arouse or cause the attitude; it was aroused by something else and then released in the judgment or attitude about the particular thing in question. [31] In order for an attitude about *x* to be objectively correct (i.e., such that it would be a mistake for anyone to hold an incompatible attitude about *x*) it must be the case that *x* could arouse the attitude in any ideal observer. We are not entitled to conclude that all moral judgments that involve emotional displacement are incorrect or mistaken. However, we are entitled to conclude that a moral judgment or attitude is incorrect *if it could only be maintained* by someone who has displaced emotions. The foregoing shows that an attitude about something is incorrect if it could not have been *caused in the appropriate way*. Consider the

Nazi's intense hatred for Jews. This is a case of displaced hostility.
His anger and hatred were caused by other things and then vented
against the Jews. We are not justified in saying that the Nazi's
attitudes are incorrect simply by appealing to facts about the
actual causes of his attitudes. But, presumably, it's not just the
case that the Nazi's attitudes were, in fact, the result of displaced
hostility; these attitudes could *only* have come about as a result of
causes other than the actions of the Jews themselves. So, we can
say that his attitudes about the Jews are incorrect because they
could not have been caused in the appropriate way; nothing that
Jews have actually done could arouse such hatred in an ideal
observer who is fully informed, etc.

We have seen that there are reasons for saying that the displacement of unfavorable emotions can distort our moral judgments.
It is at least possible that moral judgments could be distorted by a
displacement of positive emotions. For example, we might say
that a person who is extremely happy about a recent success or
madly in love may transfer his overflowing love or positive feelings
into excessively favorable judgments about the state of the world.
Such a person might not be well qualified to think about the
problem of evil.[32]

2.3.6. *The Views and Attitudes of an Ideal Observer Cannot In-volve Self-Deception*

According to Nietzsche and Scheler *ressentiment* not only "distorts" our normative judgments through emotional displacement,
it also distorts them by causing us to take a sour grapes attitude
towards certain things that we "really" desire and by causing us to
deceive ourselves into thinking that we are pleased with things
with which we are compelled to make do ('making a virtue of
necessity' or 'making something sweet out of a lemon'). I will
attempt to give reasons for requiring that the views and attitudes

of the ideal observer not involve sour grapes or making a virtue of necessity. Before doing this, however, it would be helpful to have before us paradigm cases of sour grapes and sweet lemon. Suppose that after repeated failure to achieve distinction and wealth *A* consoles himself with the thought that worldly success and the concern for it are undesirable since they distract one's attention away from reflection on "higher things". This case is a paradigm of 'sour grapes'. For an example of a normative judgment that involves making a virtue of necessity (or making something sweet out of a lemon), one cannot improve on Nietzsche's example of the man (let us call him '*B*') who although consumed by feelings of hatred and revenge never expresses anger or takes vengeance on account of general cowardice. He may baptize his cowardice, "patience", "forebearance", and "forgiveness", and come to regard it as the noblest of virtues.[33]

We might be tempted to say that these normative judgments are insincere and that the two individuals in question are self-deceived about the nature of their own values. *A* "really" attaches great value to earthly success and *B* "really" attaches little value to forebearance. The claim that *A* and *B* are self-deceived about the nature of their own normative views is problematic and cannot be assessed in the absence of a full answer to the difficult question of what is involved in accepting a normative judgment.

In any case, however, it is clear that these two cases involve some sort of self-deception. At the very least, *A* and *B* are each self-deceived about the nature of their own desires and preferences. At some level, *A* believes that he would prefer that he not have worldly success, even if it were within his power to achieve it. *B* believes that he would prefer that he not express hostility or take revenge, even if he were capable of doing so. It is part of the very concept of 'a sour grapes attitude' or 'making a virtue of necessity' that they involve this kind of self-deception. An individual who would prefer to do without something, even if he could easily have it if he wanted, cannot be said to take a sour grapes attitude in making an unfavorable evaluation of it.

Sour grapes attitudes and those that make a virtue of necessity are dependent on one's engaging in self-deception. A person who takes a sour grapes attitude about something could not persist in his unfavorable feelings and attitudes about it if he were fully aware of the nature of his own preferences, which include that he would choose to have the thing in question if possible. Similarly, the person whose favorable feelings and attitudes about something involve making a virtue of necessity, could not persist in those attitudes if he were aware of the nature of his own preferences. An ideal observer must have a clear and unconfused knowledge of all of the relevant information, including information about the nature of his own preferences.[34] This requirement precludes the possibility that he could have attitudes that involve sour grapes or making a virtue of necessity. It might be objected that a person who was fully informed about the nature of his own preferences (even an ideal observer) could have such attitudes if he regarded his own desires and preferences as being incorrect. For example, A might be forced to concede that he desires earthly success but still persist in the view that earthly success is bad. (This requires that he consider this desire to be incorrect.) However, such cases are not possible. In order for A to persist in his unfavorable assessment of worldly success in the face of the knowledge that he desires it very much, it is necessary that he believe that his desire is incorrect. But an ideal observer cannot believe that his own desires are incorrect. For he cannot have any false beliefs and if the IOT is true the correctness of attitudes is determined by the desires and attitudes that an ideal observer would have; the attitudes and desires of an ideal observer cannot be mistaken.

One might wish to formulate the IOT so as to rule out the possibility that an ideal observer could accept any moral judgments or any other views as to the correctness or incorrectness of attitudes. On the view under consideration the correctness of moral judgments about something is determined by the "natural" attitudes that it would arouse in someone under ideal conditions without his being influenced by any views to the effect that certain attitudes are correct or incorrect. I have no objection to this formulation of the IOT. On the other hand, I know of no reason for preferring it to those that permit an ideal observer to accept any moral judgments and other beliefs about the correctness of attitudes that are consistent with his other essential features. In any case, the IOT does not allow for the possibility that an ideal observer could have attitudes that involve sour grapes or making a virtue of necessity. For the only kinds of cases of sour grapes or making a virtue of necessity that could conceivably arise (given knowledge of the nature of one's own preferences) would be ones in which one believes that one's preferences are incorrect and it is precisely such beliefs that are excluded by the present formulation of the IOT.

2.3.7. An Ideal Observer Must Be a Human Being

In his arguments to show that ideal observers would all agree in their reactions concerning at least some moral issues, Firth appeals to certain facts about human psychology and thus presupposes that an ideal observer must be a human being. Without some such requirement it is clear that the IOT cannot support any kind of objectivist view. For there are absolutely no moral issues concerning which there would be unanimous agreement (either in attitudes or judgments) among all possible creatures who are fully informed and capable of vividly representing all of the relevant facts, etc. For any view or attitude, however absurd or objectionable, one can easily conceive of a possible creature who knows all of the relevant facts, etc., and who holds the view or attitude in question. It thus seems clear that the conception of an ideal observer can, at most, provide criteria for the correctness of the views and attitudes of human beings. Thus the IOT does not allow us to say that moral judgments are correct in the strong sense that we ordinarily take empirical judgments to be. For example, we take the claim that the earth is round to entail that it would be incorrect for any rational being to deny that it is round. Proponents of the ideal observer theory cannot hold that moral judgments are correct in this way. To see that this is so consider the following example. Suppose that there were Martians who, aside from not being human, possessed all of the other characteristics of ideal observers. Suppose also that the views and attitudes of the Martians differed from those of human ideal observers on numerous matters. From the standpoint of the ideal observer theory there is no reason to prefer the views of the one to the other. Rather we must conclude that the views or attitudes of the Martian ideal observers are correct for the Martians and that the views or attitudes of human ideal observers are true for us.[35] (The requirements for being a Martian ideal observer are just the same as those for being a human ideal observer, except that one must be a Martian rather than a human.)

2.3.8. *An Ideal Observer Need Not Be Impartial, Disinterested, or Dispassionate*

Firth requires that an ideal observer be impartial or disinterested. By this he means that an ideal observer cannot have any intrinsic desires for states of affairs that involve essential reference to particular things, i.e., he cannot desire those states of affairs for their own sake. An ideal observer cannot desire such things as Smith's happiness unless this desire is *entirely* dependent on a desire for the happiness of all creatures or a desire for some other state of affairs whose description involves no essential reference to any particular things.

Firth argues that when analyzing the meaning of a term one should consider the procedures that we take to be relevant to determining whether the term applies to something.

In analyzing ethical statements, for example, we must try to determine the characteristics of an ideal observer by examining the procedures which we actually regard, implicitly or explicitly, as the rational ones for *deciding* ethical questions. These procedures, to mention just a few, might include religious exercises, the acquisition of certain kinds of factual information, appeals to a moral authority, and attempts to suppress one's emotions if they are thought to be prejudicial. Each of these procedures will suggest certain characteristics of an ideal observer.[36]

Since we take an impartial perspective to be necessary for a rational inquiry into the question 'is x right?' or 'is x good?', the meaning of 'x is right' and 'x is good' must, in some way, be analyzed in terms of impartiality. Let us grant Firth his assumption — the conclusion still does not follow. In general, the fact that we take a certain procedure, p, to be reliable for determining whether something is t does not entail that the ultimate analysis of t must include some reference to p. p may simply be taken to be a reliable procedure for determining the presence of some further characteristic, x, in terms of which t is to be defined. The data to which Firth appeals is compatible with alternative analyses of moral notions. It is, for example, compatible with the Brentanist theory, according to which moral judgments are statements about the correctness of attitudes. Given the Brentanist Theory, one could still consider the notion of an ideal observer to be a reliable guide for determining the correctness of attitudes. However, on this view the claim that an ideal observer must be impartial cannot be justified simply by appeal to our ordinary ways of thinking about these issues — perhaps we are mistaken in thinking that impartiality has anything to do with the correctness of attitudes. One needs to demonstrate some connection between being impartial and having correct attitudes.

None of the foregoing counts in favor of the view that the notion of an ideal observer formulated as a criterion for the correctness of attitudes must include a requirement about impartiality. Let us assume that Firth's claims about the meaning of moral terms are correct, i.e., that in making a moral judgment about something one is claiming that all people who are fully informed and impartial, etc., would have a certain sort of attitude about it. Suppose that a certain act A is morally wrong in Firth's sense, i.e., assume that any ideal observer would have an unfavorable attitude about it. Suppose also that S who is fully informed but does not view A impartially has a favorable (or at least not an unfavorable) attitude about A and claims that it is morally permissible. (It might help to suppose that act A is S's successfully embezzling money from a bank.) If Firth is correct, then S is simply mistaken in holding that A is permissible. However, we still would have no basis for saying that it is incorrect for S to have a favorable attitude about A. The fact that an attitude would not be held by anyone who was fully informed and impartial does not (by itself) show that the attitude in question is, in any sense, mistaken or incorrect. In order to draw this conclusion validly one would need to give reasons for thinking that attitudes that are dependent on one's being partial or having desires that involve essential reference to particular things are incorrect. I simply don't know of any good reasons given by Firth or anyone else for supposing that this is so.

One could argue that since it is true that A is wrong it follows that it is incorrect for anyone to have a favorable attitude about A. Or, more generally, since assuming the moral point of view involves being impartial,[37] attitudes that are essentially partial are incorrect. I agree that something's being wrong implies that it is incorrect to have a favorable attitude about it. But this does not show that S's approval of A is mistaken, but only that Firth's analysis of moral terms is mistaken. For, given his view, to say that something is right or wrong etc., does not necessarily imply that it is correct to have a favorable or unfavorable attitude about it.

Firth makes a strong case for thinking that his theory is a correct account of what we mean in our everyday moral judgments. But, even if his theory were a correct account of meaning, that would not permit us to conclude that it is an acceptable standard for determining the correctness of attitudes. Firth's theory cannot provide us with any answer to an amoralist who claims that it is in no sense mistaken or incorrect for him to be indifferent to moral considerations. Suppose that an amoral mass-murderer comes to accept Firth's theory and as a result admits that what he does is morally wrong in this sense. He could still say the following: "Mass murder is wrong in your sense of 'wrong', but so what? Why should I care that what I do would be disapproved of by someone who was fully informed and impartial, etc.? Why should I be impartial?" I want to construct a version of the IOT that is capable of offering a reply to the amoralist's query — a theory that could show that his attitudes are incorrect or inappropriate. Given this aim, and given my inability to discover any convincing links between the notions of impartiality and the correctness of attitudes (unlike false beliefs or incomplete information partiality is not an error or cognitive defect in any obvious sense), I do not think that the requirement that an ideal observer be impartial can be justified. This is to be regretted since the theory would be much stronger if it were possible to justify such a requirement. (See Section 2.4.)

Essentially the same sorts of things can be said about the condition that an ideal observer must be dispassionate and I shall also drop this feature from the description of the ideal observer.

2.3.9. An Ideal Observer Need Not Be "Normal"

Firth's requirement that an ideal observer be "normal" in all respects other than those having to do with his omniscience and other essential features is open to serious objections. The purpose of this condition, I take it, is to rule out certain kinds of unusual mental characteristics that might cause an ideal observer to make judgments or hold attitudes that are inconsistent with those of other ideal observers. One might take the condition that an ideal observer must be normal to mean that he cannot be mentally ill. However, the concepts of mental health and mental illness are irreducibly normative or evaluative. Mental illness is by definition something that is undesirable or bad for one. Interpreted in this way, the requirement that an ideal observer must be normal contains illicit normative assumptions and must be dispensed with if the theory is to serve its avowed aim of constituting an ultimate standard or criterion for normative views.

Perhaps a more accurate reading of 'normal' is 'common or ordinary in some statistical sense'.[38] Firth still does not indicate how the condition is to be interpreted in order to determine which sorts of characteristics are excluded by being normal. In the absence of clarification on these points and the absence of any arguments for thinking that being "normal" (in whatever sense is proposed) has any essential connection with the correctness of our attitudes, I feel justified in assuming that this condition should be dropped.

2.4. THREE VERSIONS OF THE IDEAL OBSERVER THEORY AND THEIR IMPLICATIONS FOR THE OBJECTIVITY OF MORAL JUDGMENTS

Using the conception of the ideal observer developed in Section 2.3, I will now formulate three versions of the ideal observer theory which I take to be plausible and two of which seem to support at least a minimal version of moral objectivism.

2.4.1. *The Version of the IOT According to Which the Correctness of a Moral Judgment Is Determined by Its Acceptability to Ideal Observers*

Consider the following:

(I)   A particular moral judgment is true for all human beings if, and only if, all human ideal observers would accept it.

The implications of (I) depend very importantly on the kind of moral training that we attribute to an ideal observer. There are two main possibilities: (a) we could say that an ideal observer has received no moral training at all and has no acquaintance with representative moral concepts and theories (this rules out the possibility that he could have the kind of knowledge of relevant moral principles discussed earlier in this chapter (Section 2.3.3)), or (b) we could say that an ideal observer can have received any kind of moral training and have any kind of acquaintance with moral notions that is compatible with his other essential features, i.e., anything that did not involve the acceptance of false beliefs or the ignorance of relevant facts. There are other alternatives, but these are the only plausible ones. Surely it would be a mistake to require that all ideal observers be trained in any particular moral view or to require that they have an acquaintance with some particular moral concepts and theories but not others. If we suppose that the ideal observer has no moral training, then (I) is likely to lead to an extreme version of relativism according to which there are no moral judgments that are objectively correct. For a person who has received no moral training is likely not to be moved to make any moral judgments at all. It seems extremely unlikely that any sizable group of such individuals would all agree in their judgments about any moral issues. (b) does not improve things much, for, given (b), there could still be ideal observers

who have no moral training at all — this is a possibility that is
compatible with their possessing all of the other essential characteristics of an ideal observer. It is possible that some of the ideal
observers who have received no moral training would make no
moral judgments. It is also likely that some of the ideal observers
who have received no moral training would be moral nihilists and
make no moral judgments on that account. We can't say that this
possibility is ruled out, because the IOT supports objectivism. For
the question at issue is whether it does support objectivism. It is
still likely that there are some issues, e.g., genocide, concerning
which all ideal observers who venture to make moral judgments
would all agree. Whether this is an adequate basis for claiming the
objectivity of at least some moral issues is a question that I shall
not pursue here, since there seem to be other versions of the IOT
that are more promising in this regard.

2.4.2. The Version of the IOT According to Which the Correct-ness of a Moral Judgment About Something Is Determined by the Attitudes that Ideal Observers Would Have About It

The following alternative formulation of the IOT takes the attitudes of an ideal observer (rather than the judgments that he
accepts) to be the standard for determining the correctness of
moral judgments.

(II)   A favorable moral judgment about something is correct
         for all human beings if and only if all human ideal
         observers would have a favorable attitude about it. An
         unfavorable moral judgment about something is true or
         correct for all human beings if and only if all human
         ideal observers would have an unfavorable attitude
         about it. If all ideal observers would be indifferent to
         something, then it is correct (in a sense that is opposed
         to mistaken) for all humans to be indifferent to it. If

different ideal observers would have conflicting attitudes about x, some having a favorable attitude about it, some having an unfavorable attitude, and others being indifferent, then there is no moral judgment about x that is correct for all human beings.[39]

Note that I only present the ideal observer theory as a standard for the correctness of moral judgments. Unlike Firth, I do not propose the theory as an analysis of what we *mean* when we make moral judgments. We can distinguish between standards for the correctness of judgments of right and good and bad and wrong along the lines suggested in Chapter One. As stated, (II) leaves open the possibility that a certain sort of attitude about something could be correct (in a sense that is opposed to mistaken) for a particular individual, even if it is not correct for all human beings. (For example, one might say that it would be incorrect for someone to have a favorable attitude about abortion, even if it would not be incorrect for all other human beings to have a favorable attitude about abortion.) Let me stipulate that (II) should be understood to exclude this possibility. So, (II) implies that it can't be correct in a sense that is opposed to incorrect for *an individual* to have a certain attitude about something unless it is correct in a sense that is opposed to mistaken for *all human beings* to have that attitude. I will later consider a formulation of the IOT that allows that an attitude can be correct (in a sense that is opposed to mistaken) for an individual even if not for all human beings.

2.4.3. *Some Difficulties with the Second Version of the IOT*

There remain many features of this formulation of the IOT that stand in need of justification and explanation. Assuming that the attitudes of ideal observers should constitute our ultimate criterion for the correctness of moral judgments, I take it that there is no problem with (II) as a criterion for the correctness of favorable and unfavorable moral judgments. If a favorable (unfavorable) moral judgment is true for all human beings, then failing to have a favorable (unfavorable) attitude about it constitutes a kind of mistake or error and someone who did not make any errors (an ideal observer) could not fail to have a favorable (unfavorable) attitude about it. However, the remaining portion of (II) is very much open to dispute. (II) is what I call an 'attitude version' of the IOT in that it takes the attitudes of ideal observers (as opposed to their beliefs or judgments) to be the ultimate standard for the correctness of moral judgments. The general thrust of 'attitude' versions of the IOT commits us to saying that if all ideal observers would share a particular sort of attitude about something, then that attitude must be correct for all human beings. We are thus committed to saying that if all ideal observers would be indifferent to something then it must be correct (in a sense that is opposed to mistaken) for everyone to be indifferent to it. As we saw in Chapter One (Section 1.1.2), this is not equivalent to saying that the thing in question is morally indifferent. To say that something is morally indifferent is to say that any kind of attitude about it is correct, i.e., that no attitude about it can be mistaken. There is no moral concept in our language corresponding to the possibility envisaged in (II), i.e., no moral concept that we can apply to something to indicate that indifference is the only attitude that it is correct to have about it. To claim that there are things concerning which indifference is the only correct attitude conflicts with a principle that is *prima facie* plausible, namely, that if it is correct to be indifferent to something then it must also be correct to have a favorable attitude about it (see Chapter One). The name that I gave to this principle, 'the non-killjoy principle', suggests strong grounds for accepting it. However, I think that the general sorts of considerations that moved us to accept the IOT should convince us to give up this principle if necessary. For, if all ideal observers would be indifferent to something (there is no reason to think that such a case could not arise), then one's having any other sort of attitude about it must be the result of some kind of error or cognitive failing.

It might be objected that the analysis of moral judgments defended in Chapter One suggests that we take the fact that different ideal observers would have the full range of different and opposed attitudes (favorable, unfavorable and neutral) about something to be evidence, not for the claim that there is no objectively correct moral judgment concerning it, but rather for the claim that it is objectively true that the thing is question is morally indifferent. My criteria for the correctness of favorable and unfavorable moral judgments make use of the following principle: 'an attitude about x is incorrect if and only if no ideal observers would (could) have that particular attitude about x'. If something is such that different ideal observers could have favorable, unfavorable, or neutral attitudes about it, then no attitude about it can be incorrect (i.e., any attitude about it is correct), and, therefore, it must be morally indifferent. (To say that something is morally indifferent is to say that any kind of attitude about it can be correct.)

It is important for my argument in the next chapter to be able to describe this as a case in which there is no correct judgment. The answer to the foregoing objection is that, given the analysis of moral judgments defended in Chapter One, and given that a particular person's attitude about x cannot be correct in a sense that is opposed to mistaken unless that attitude is also correct for all other human beings (this is a stipulation of (II)), then it follows that 'x is morally indifferent' and 'there is no moral judgment that it is correct (*in a sense that is opposed to mistaken*) for one to have about x' have precisely the same truth conditions. Both entail and are entailed by the following: 'any attitude about x can be correct (*in the sense of not being mistaken*)'.

One final problem with (II) is that the possibilities for agreement and disagreement in attitude that it mentions are not exhaustive. In addition, there are the following three possibilities: (1) Some ideal observers have a favorable attitude about x, some have an unfavorable attitude, and none are indifferent; (2) some have a favorable attitude, some are indifferent, and none have an unfavorable attitude; and (3) some have an unfavorable attitude, some are indifferent, and none have a favorable attitude. I suggest that we treat these possibilities along the same lines as the possibility that all ideal observers would be indifferent to something and use the following principle: if there is an attitude about something that no possible ideal observer would (could) have, then that attitude is incorrect for all human beings.

2.4.4. *What Counts as a Favorable or Unfavorable Attitude?*

It is incumbent upon me to make clear what I mean by 'favorable' and 'unfavorable' attitudes. This also raises many difficult issues, so, it will be necessary to enter into another long digression here. Favorable and unfavorable attitudes can manifest themselves in either actions or feelings (or dispositions to act or feel). The fact that a person has or is disposed to have favorable emotions about something, e.g., feel pleased or satisfied with it, counts in favor of the claim that he has a favorable attitude about it. The fact that a person is disposed to choose to promote the occurrence or existence of something also counts in favor of the claim that he has a favorable attitude about it. The same remarks apply to unfavorable attitudes.

There are many common kinds of cases in which we would expect an ideal observer to have 'mixed' feelings or conflicting attitudes about something. For example, when contemplating the choice of a nation's leaders to wage war rather than submit to tyranny the natural sympathies of an ideal observer would pull him in the direction of both favor and disfavor. In order to deal adequately with such cases we need to find criteria for determining whether mixed attitudes are favorable or unfavorable *on the whole*. I propose that we take facts about how a person acts and is disposed to act to be decisive in determining the favorableness or unfavorableness of his attitudes. A person's attitudes about something are favorable on the whole if, and only if, he would prefer (choose) its existence or occurrence to its non-existence or non-occurrence, everything else being equal. His attitudes are unfavorable on the whole if and only if he would prefer its non-existence or non-occurrence to its existence or occurrence, everything else being equal. For example, if I have conflicting emotions about the world economic system that gives me an income 170 times as great as that of the average citizen of India, but would still choose to continue that kind of inequality even if it were within my power to change it, then we must say that, all things considered, I have a favorable attitude about the way in which the world's wealth is divided.

Firth takes a very different approach to the issue of which attitudes and reactions of an ideal observer are to be considered relevant to determining the correctness of moral judgments. He does not consider any kind of favorable or unfavorable attitude to be ethically significant – but only those that are characterized by what he calls a "demand quality". This is a crucial difference between his theory and my own. I will first indicate certain welcome consequences that follow from Firth's restriction and then offer my reasons for preferring my own view to his.

It seems likely that Firth's restriction of ethically relevant reactions to those that involve some kind of demand quality will insure a greater measure of unanimity in what are judged to be the ethically significant reactions of ideal observers and thus also support a stronger version of objectivism. I have in mind the following kind of case. Gestapo agent X kills Y under the threat of punishment or for the sake of worldly gain. Given my way of determining what counts as a favorable or unfavorable attitude, it is unlikely that all ideal observers would have an unfavorable attitude about X's killing Y (would choose to have him not kill Y), because some of them could conceivably be in the position of X or someone else who stands to gain from this action. (My theory dispenses with the requirement of impartiality and does nothing to rule out this possibility.) Even if all ideal observers wouldn't choose that X refrain from killing Y, they might all feel that it is 'required' that he so refrain. Thus, even without the requirement of impartiality, Firth may be able to claim that it is objectively correct to say that it was wrong for X to kill Y.

Firth's account of the "morally significant" attitudes of ideal observers also allows for an intuitively plausible account of the concept of moral indifference and it enables us to make a clear distinction between things that are morally indifferent and things concerning which there is no objectively correct moral judgment. According to Firth, a favorable (unfavorable) moral judgment about x is objectively true if, and only if, all ideal observers would have a favorable (unfavorable) attitude (characterized by a demand quality) about x. Although he doesn't offer any definite proposals on this point, Firth would presumably want to say that the morally indifferent is that which would not arouse any attitudes that are characterized by a demand quality in ideal observers. Note that this allows for the possibility that something could be morally indifferent, even if many ideal observers would have desires and aversions with respect to it. Something would count as morally indifferent provided that none of the attitudes of ideal observers would be characterized by a demand quality. For example, it might be the case that some ideal observers would have desires and aversions with respect to eating chocolate chip ice cream, but presumably none of these desires or aversions would be characterized by a demand quality. In that case Firth could say that eating chocolate chip ice cream is morally indifferent. If there would be disagreement in attitude among ideal observers, and if at least some of their attitudes would be characterized by a demand quality, then, on Firth's view, it seems most plausible to count it as an issue concerning which there is no objectively correct moral judgment. (Although I am reasonably certain that this is what he would say about this case, Firth himself does not consider this possibility.)

In spite of these noteworthy virtues, I believe that there are reasons for preferring my approach to Firth's.

(a) Even if we grant that some kind of demand quality is a unique feature of certain morally significant experiences, it could conceivably be the case that such experiences are essentially a product of conventional moral training. It may be the case that a person who had no acquaintance with moral notions (this is compatible with Firth's description of the ideal observer) would never have experiences that involved any kind of demand quality. (This itself would be enough to destroy the unanimity of the ideal observers' reactions.)

(b) Our experiences are often characterized by a demand quality when reflecting on questions of right and wrong but this does not seem to be the case with questions of good and bad. Consider the sort of case in which one says that a certain action is morally wrong, even though it has better consequences than any of its alternatives. Typically, only the former sort of judgment is backed up by any feeling of demand. Adopting Firth's view that only experiences characterized by this demand quality are ethically significant makes it difficult to see how the IOT can function as a standard for the correctness of judgments of good and bad.

(c) Last, and most importantly, Firth's theory leaves open the question of why one should pay greater heed to those experiences that are characterized by a demand quality than those that are not. Suppose that someone is thinking of committing a murder in order to gain a considerable sum of money and is torn between greed and empathy for the victim. On the whole, he may be more strongly inclined to commit the murder rather than not, even though only his desire not to kill the man is characterized by any demand quality. Why should he act on the desire that is characterized by the demand quality? Why is it in any sense mistaken or irrational for him to act on his strongest desires rather than those that are characterized by a demand quality? Firth's theory can provide no answers to these kinds of questions, which might be raised by a radical moral skeptic or relativist. I want to construct a theory that can provide an answer to such questions. On my view, the question 'Why should I give special preference to my "moral" desires (those that are characterized by a demand quality or those that are impartial) over other desires?' does not arise. For, on my view, the correct attitude for me to have about something is simply the overall attitude that I would have if I were fully informed and fully rational, etc. The morally right action for one to perform is the action that a fully informed and fully rational person would be most strongly inclined to perform in that situation. Here, I should say a bit more about the implications of my theory for the question, 'why be moral?' Suppose that all ideal observers would prefer that S do x in a certain situation. Then, according to (II), the claim that S ought to do x is true for all human beings. Couldn't S still ask, "why should I care? Why should I do what I or anyone else would do in my position if I (he) were fully rational?" This is tantamount to asking, 'why should I be rational?' or 'why should I do the rational thing (the rational thing being what I would do if I were fully rational)?' The theory defended in this book affords no special way of justifying rationality and no way of motivating people to be rational. My argument only purports to show that there is a connection between rational and being moral.

2.4.5. The Implications of the Second Version of the IOT for Questions About the Objectivity of Morals

Let us return from these lengthy digressions to a consideration of the implications of the second formulation of the IOT (II) for questions about the objectivity of moral judgments. It is very unlikely that ideal observers would agree in their attitudes about all conceivable moral questions, for the essential features of an ideal observer are simply not sufficient to determine his attitudes about all conceivable moral issues. Thus it seems unlikely that (II) can support a strong version of moral objectivism. However, I believe that (II) supports a weak version of objectivism according to which there are judgments concerning at least some moral issues that are correct for all human beings. At the very least, all human ideal observers would have unfavorable attitudes about wars of conquest, mass murder, and other acts that cause gratuitous suffering. No human ideal observer could fail to have a favorable attitude about most ordinary kinds of sexual activity and sexual pleasure. I am assuming that human beings have a natural tendency to respond sympathetically to the sufferings of other creatures provided that they (1) represent adequately the experiences of other creatures and (2) do not displace anger or hatred in contemplating the situation of others. Given these assumptions, it follows that no one who satisfied the conditions for being an ideal observer could fail to be displeased by gratuitous suffering or to be pleased by gratuitous happiness.

There are several kinds of cases that might seem to constitute counter-examples to this. The most difficult are those that involve malice or sadism. There are plainly people who enjoy the contemplation of other people's suffering and who enjoy inflicting pain on them. I need to argue that malicious people either displace hostility or fail to represent adequately the feelings of other creatures or both. There is a strong *prima facie* case for this view.

Malicious conduct is frequently, if not characteristically, an outlet for free floating hostility. Malicious people often fail to represent adequately the feelings of other people and they often feel remorse if they bring the sufferings of others vividly to mind. That a sadist derives pleasure from the outward manifestations of another person's suffering — his cries, pleas, and writhing, etc., does not show that he derives pleasure from a vivid awareness of other people's suffering.

Even if a person derives no pleasure or satisfaction from heinous acts, he may still engage in them or be favorably disposed towards them if they provide him with sufficient worldly gain. This kind of situation creates problems for my version of the IOT, since an ideal observer could conceivably be favorably disposed towards terrible acts for the sake of worldly gain. For example, a person might choose to allow the Nazis to deprive the Jews of their rights in order to acquire Jewish property. My theory is in grave danger of reverting to extreme relativism if ideal observers could approve of such things as genocide for these sorts of reasons. For it does not rule out the possibility that an ideal observer could be in a position to derive worldly gain from such things. In such situations, the vast majority of people find that they cannot perpetrate or acquiesce in evil without first averting their eyes or hardening their hearts to the sufferings of others.[40] I am inclined to think that a non-rancorous person could not condone mass-murder for the sake of worldly gain without hardening his heart. This would be enough to snatch the IOT from the jaws of extreme relativism, but an adequate defense of this would require much more than the appeal to armchair psychology that I am able to offer here.[41]

At the very worst, I think that all ideal observers would disapprove of gratuitously harmful acts. At best, I doubt that they would all agree in requiring any acts that require significant self-sacrifice on the part of the agent. For at least some of the possible ideal observers would be in the position of the persons who are called upon to make the sacrifices, and there is nothing in our conception of the ideal observer that requires that he be disposed to make sacrifices for the sake of others (or feel disapproval for those who fail to make such sacrifices). An ideal observer would not necessarily have an unfavorable attitude about the actions of a soldier who carried out an order to massacre innocent civilians if the soldier ran the risk of being killed, himself, for not following orders. However, in this case, all ideal observers would presumably share an unfavorable attitude about whoever is ultimately responsible for issuing the orders. If the reader is inclined to be dissatisfied with this result I can only say that I agree. I would *like* to defend a much stronger view than this, but I believe that this is the strongest position that can be defended.

Given some additional requirement to the effect that an ideal observer must be impartial, the IOT would support a much stronger version of objectivism. The sort of impartiality that Firth attributes to the ideal observer would be enough to insure that an ideal observer would never be moved to favor such things as genocide for reasons of self-interest. (According to Firth, an ideal observer cannot have a desire for his own personal welfare or the welfare of any other particular individual.) A stronger conception of impartiality such as Rawls's would insure that ideal observers would have very strong self-interested reasons for disapproving of the extermination of any particular group of people. For, given this condition, an ideal observer could never be certain that he was not a member of the group whose extermination was being contemplated.

Given a condition of impartiality strong enough to insure that ideal observers would have no preference for promoting their own welfare over that of others, the IOT might seem to support utilitarianism. For benevolence and the concern for one's own welfare seem to be natural human desires and it seems at least plausible to say that such desires as the desire to be honest and

keep promises (even when doing so will not have the best consequences) are 'artificial' desires that are the product of moral
training. A natural human being who was untainted by moral
training or emotional displacement, constrained by a strong
condition of impartiality, and who adequately represented the
experiences of other people would act and react just as someone
whose actions and emotions were in perfect accordance with the
principle of utility. However, there are serious problems with this
line of reasoning. Even if benevolence is the only other-regarding
virtue that has an instinctive basis in human nature, an ideal
observer could conceivably come to have an intrinsic desire to
tell the truth and keep promises, etc., as a result of doing those
things for utilitarian reasons in just the same way that many
people come to desire money or professional success for their
own sake as a consequence of pursuing them for the sake of
other things. I have a vague suspicion that desires acquired in
this way rest on a certain kind of confusion of means and ends
and are thus irrational. If one could make out a case for thinking
that acquiring desires in this way is incompatible with one's
being an ideal observer, then (given a strong condition of impartiality) the IOT would seem to support utilitarianism. However,
if an ideal observer can acquire desires in the way that a miser
acquires his desire for money then, the IOT does not support
utilitarianism.

2.4.6. The IOT as a Standard for the Correctness of an Individual Person's Moral Judgments

The IOT can also be formulated as a criterion for the correctness
of an individual person's moral judgments:

(III)   It is correct (in a sense that is opposed to mistaken) for
          S to accept a favorable (unfavorable) moral judgment

about x if, and only if, S would have a favorable (unfavorable) attitude about x if he possessed all of the
essential features of an ideal observer. It is correct (in
a sense that is opposed to mistaken) for S to judge that
x is morally indifferent if, and only if, S would be indifferent to x, if he possessed all of the essential characteristics of an ideal observer and everything else were
the same.[42]

'If one possessed all of the essential features of an ideal observer
and everything else were the same' should be understood to imply
'if one had all of the essential features of an ideal observer and one
had all of one's actual wants and aversions except for those that
are dependent on one's having had false beliefs or incomplete
information'.

My formulation of (III) seems to presuppose that the expression
'S as he would be if he were an ideal observer and everything else
were the same' picks out a determinate state of affairs so that the
statement 'S would have a favorable attitude about x if he were
an ideal observer and everything else were the same' has a definite
truth value. However, this is far from clear. We can imagine an
almost infinite number of possible life-histories of a particular
person in which he becomes an ideal observer. It's not clear that
there is any particular one of these life-histories that has a claim
to be called the one that is 'most similar to the person's actual life'
or the one in which 'everything else is the same as in his present
life'. I shall not attempt to resolve any of the notoriously difficult
questions concerning the interpretation of counterfactual statements. I will simply try to take cognizance of this problem.
Suppose that the assumption incorporated in (III) is false. Suppose
that there are statements of the form 'S would have a favorable
(unfavorable) attitude about x if he were an ideal observer and
everything else were the same', which have no definite truth value.

In this case, we should take (III) to imply that there is no moral judgment concerning x that is true for S. Suppose that there are no statements of this form that have a definite truth value. In that unlikely case, (III) would entail that there are no moral judgments about anything that are true for anyone. ((II) would also have this consequence in such a case.)

There are important differences between (III) and our earlier versions of the IOT. The most obvious differences arise in connection with issues concerning which ideal observers would not all agree. It is very likely that some ideal observers would approve (and others disapprove) of lying to a very sick patient about the seriousness of his condition in order to spare him the ill-effects of the fright that this knowledge would occasion. (I) and (II) imply that there is no objectively correct moral judgment (or judgment that is correct for all human beings) concerning this issue. (III) also implies that there is no one view about this question that is correct for *everyone* to hold. (I) and (II) imply that if there is no objectively correct view about a given question, then it is completely arbitrary what one believes about it. (I) and (II) also imply that one could never be mistaken in believing one thing about it as opposed to another. (III), however, does not have this consequence. It implies that it can be correct (in a sense that is opposed to mistaken) for a person to accept a particular moral judgment, even if that judgment is not objectively correct. Suppose that you would approve of lying to the sick patient in our example if you had all of the characteristics of an ideal observer; suppose, also, that I would disapprove of lying to him if I were an ideal observer. (III) implies that it is correct for me to hold views that it would be incorrect for you to hold.

There are several respects in which (III) is attractive to those who wish to defend as much as possible of our common sense moral views. As we have seen, on any defensible characterization of the ideal observer, there are apt to be a great many issues concerning which ideal observers would not all agree. Unlike the other versions of the IOT, (III) does not imply that it is completely arbitrary what an individual believes about those issues or that his views are not subject to rational criticism. Suppose that there are no moral issues concerning which ideal observers would all agree. Among other things, (II) would imply that it is not objectively correct to hold that genocide is wrong. This would be an extremely disconcerting result for those who accept the IOT. However, it is somewhat less distressing given (III). For given (III), we can still say that it is correct for *us* (and almost everyone else, including all or most Nazis) to disapprove of Nazism, since *we* surely would have an unfavorable attitude about it if *we* possessed the characteristics of an ideal observer.

One possible difficulty with (III) is that it makes the class of things that are morally indifferent much narrower than we ordinarily take it to be. We often regard the objects of our whims and preferences, e.g., my preference that the sum of the numbers on the jerseys of the players on the field be divisible by 29, to be morally indifferent. (III) commits us to saying that it's true for me that such states of affairs are good or bad provided that my desires or aversions with respect to them would persist if I became an ideal observer. Clearly the fact that I would persist in my aversion to its being the case that the number of hairs on your head is divisible by 3 if I were an ideal observer provides us no basis for saying that it is objectively true that it is good that the number of hairs on your head be divisible by 3. From an objective point of view, this is clearly an indifferent state of affairs. But there is nothing objectionable about saying that it is true for a particular person (given his history and preferences, etc.) that it is good that the number of hairs on your head be divisible by 3. For we are allowing for the possibility that this would not have been true for him if his life had been different and his preferences were of a different sort than they are in fact.

2.5. SERMONETTE ON THE IMPORTANCE OF EMPATHY

I am very much struck by the inadequacy of our ordinary ways of representing other people's feelings. This inadequacy is partly a function of limitations in our powers of imagination and representation. However, the adequacy of our representations of other people's experiences is also very much a function of our own efforts. To represent the experiences of another person in even a moderately adequate way requires deliberate effort. There are many reasons why we often fail to do this.

(1) We may simply be unwilling to take the time or effort to do so. For example, in the course of my daily activities I may be unwilling to take the time to represent the plight of the children of the soldiers whose deaths are being reported in the daily news.

(2) We often find it unpleasant and disconcerting to think about the suffering of other people. Not only is it unpleasant to represent the suffering of a soldier maimed in battle, it is quite unpleasant just to look at him or hear his cries. We often avert our eyes and harden our hearts to the suffering of others simply in order to minimize our own suffering.

(3) We also fail to represent the suffering of others in order to avoid feeling guilty for not doing anything to alleviate it and also to avoid the sacrifices that we might be tempted to make if we were to represent it. For example, a member of a rich industrial society might refuse to look at pictures of destitute and starving people, or to represent their suffering to himself for fear of arousing his conscience and/or fear of being led to make sacrifices for them. (In order to represent the suffering of those who are starving to ourselves in even a moderately adequate way, we would need to spend time fasting and sleeping in the streets.)

To represent the experiences of others in a vivid and reasonably adequate way can have an enormous influence on one's attitudes and actions. It can make for more "enlightened" (or more nearly correct) attitudes and more virtuous conduct. Few, if any, human beings can picture the sorrow of the world without being moved. This raises the question of whether, and, if so, to what extent, we are obligated to represent the suffering (and joys) of other people. Clearly, we are not obligated to represent fully and adequately the suffering of other people — we cannot be obligated to do what we are unable to do. Nor is anyone obligated to represent the experiences of other people as well as it is possible for him to do, for that is an all-consuming task that would not allow any time or energy for other endeavors. However, a responsible moral agent is obligated to base his decisions on as full and as vivid an awareness of the relevant facts (including the feelings of others) as is possible, compatible with his not devoting an excessive amount of time to deliberation. We have to decide which things we will represent to ourselves and also how much effort we should devote to representing particular states of affairs. In general, we should try to represent suffering and joy which is within our power to cause or limit. We are not obligated to make ourselves miserable thinking about instances of suffering over which we have no control. For example, I should devote my energies to representing the suffering of people in impoverished nations (which I have some power to alleviate by means of private charity and political action) rather than representing the suffering of people from the black death during the Middle Ages. (I should, however, retain a dispositional knowledge of suffering which is beyond my power to do anything about.)

Morally responsible decision making about actions that may cause or relieve the suffering of others must involve a vivid awareness of the nature of that suffering, even if that awareness causes the agent considerable distress and unhappiness himself. It is not permissible for us to avert our eyes to suffering in which we ourselves are involved. I am not, however, inclined to agree with those who contend that a good person (a morally virtuous person) would have to be unhappy due to sympathy for the state of the world. A good person must have knowledge of the suffering of others, but he need not spend great portions of his time wallowing in pity for other people. He can keep his knowledge of the suffering of the world dispositional most of the time; he only needs to bring it vividly to mind when he is reflecting about what he ought to do.[43]

2.6. INTUITIONISM AND THE IDEAL OBSERVER THEORY

One of the most serious problems for intuitionist theories is the fact that people seem to have conflicting intuitions about moral questions. The fact that, for almost any moral issue, there are people who report intuitions that are greatly at variance with those of others, suggests that there aren't any objective moral truths or moral facts for us to intuit. The existence of such truths would seem to involve a greater measure of agreement than does in fact exist.

An intuitionist might try to meet this objection by appealing to the ideal observer theory. He could say that a person's intuitions are distorted by his failure to possess any of the essential characteristics of an ideal observer. The fact of disagreement does not, itself, cast any doubt on the existence of objective moral facts — it may only show that some people's intuitions are distorted or mistaken. In order for this reply to succeed, it is necessary that the intuitionist be able to give a plausible account of how one's failure to possess the features of an ideal observer distorts one's moral intuitions. Given such an explanation, the IOT can perhaps help support a modest version of objectivism according to which there are objective moral facts concerning some moral issues. However, the IOT cannot support the strong kind of objectivism usually defended by intuitionists, because, as we have seen, ideal observers could disagree in their views or intuitions about many moral questions.

Some intuitionists such as Moore hold that moral qualities are simple non-natural characteristics of a rather mysterious sort that are directly intuited. Moore does not offer a very helpful account of the nature of moral intuition. He makes much of the analogy between 'good' and 'yellow'.[44] This suggests that he takes moral intuition to be analogous to sensory experience. If this is so, then it is difficult to see how falling short of being an ideal observer could distort one's intuitions. Lacking factual knowledge and being resentful, etc., do not distort a person's perception of the color yellow. Perhaps I am misreading Moore here, but in any case we need to find a clearer account of his views about the nature of moral intuition in order to determine whether the proposed explanation of conflicting intuitions is open to him.

Ross holds that the moral characteristics of something are resultant or supervenient on its other non-moral features.[45] For example, we might say that the goodness of a person's character is entirely a function of facts about how he acts and is disposed to act. Given this, it is perhaps possible to see how false beliefs or incomplete information could distort one's intuitions. If I have false beliefs or incomplete information about something, I have not adequately represented its non-moral qualities. Since moral qualities are logically dependent on the non-moral qualities, I will also have an inadequate representation or intuition of the latter. However, it is not at all clear how one's being resentful, partial, or having had false beliefs *in the past* can distort one's intuitions on this view.

Ewing and Brentano hold that there being moral facts consists in its being the case that certain things are such that it is simply appropriate for any rational being to have certain sorts of attitudes about them.[46] On this view it is easy to see how false beliefs or incomplete information could distort one's intuitions. According to this view, a moral intuition is the perception of the fittingness of an attitude for a certain object. If an object is actually other than it is as represented by me, then I may still be able to intuit the appropriateness of a certain attitude for the thing *as I represent it*. Ewing and Brentano could thus account for the possibility of mistaken and conflicting intuitions while still holding that everyone's intuitions would be correct and in agreement if they correctly represented the things about which they make their judgments. However, their version of intuitionism still leaves it unclear how such things as emotional displacement or having been ill-informed in the past can distort one's intuitions. Unless it is possible to explain this (it's not clear that any of the versions of intuitionism considered here can do this), then it seems as if the IOT cannot resolve the intuitionist's difficulties with conflicting intuitions. For if an ideal observer is simply characterized as someone who is fully informed, then it is doubtful that all possible ideal observers would agree in their attitudes about any moral issues.

CHAPTER THREE

RELATIVISM AND NIHILISM

> "If he does really think that there is
> no distinction between vice and virtue,
> when he leaves our houses let us count
> our spoons." (*Samuel Johnson*)

In Chapter One I argued that moral judgments involve claims about the correctness of attitudes. In making a favorable (or unfavorable) moral judgment about something one is claiming that it is correct for any rational being (or at least any human being) to have a favorable (or unfavorable) attitude about it. In Chapter Two, we saw reasons for thinking that there are many moral issues (probably the overwhelming majority) concerning which there is no attitude that is correct for all human beings. There is even some chance that there are no moral issues concerning which there is an attitude that is correct in this sense. I thus seem to be committed to the view that most moral questions are such that any moral judgment concerning them is false or mistaken. Moral judgments presuppose that attitudes about things are correct in a sense in which they aren't. This view might appear to constitute a kind of nihilism or rejection of morality. In this chapter, I want to determine whether or not it is consistent for me to make moral judgments about any of those issues concerning which I believe that there is no objectively correct view or no view that is correct for all human beings. It is clear that my view denies much of what is implicitly claimed in ordinary moral judgments, and therefore it is important to determine which aspects of our ordinary moral perspective I am committed to abandoning and whether the view that I am left with is in any sense a moral one.

In Chapter One, I argued that many of the characteristic functions
of moral judgments — prescribing actions to other people and
altering their attitudes — are dependent on their purporting to be
correct, at least correct for all human beings. Moral judgments
could not serve all of these functions if everyone accepted the
version of relativism proposed in Chapter Two.

At the end of Chapter Two, I defended the following view:

(III)   It is correct (in a sense that is opposed to mistaken) for
         S to accept a favorable (unfavorable) moral judgment
         about x if, and only if, S would have a favorable (un-
         favorable) attitude about x if he possessed all of the
         essential features of an ideal observer. It is correct (in
         a sense that is opposed to mistaken) for S to judge that
         x is morally indifferent if, and only if, S would be indif-
         ferent to x, if he possessed all of the essential charac-
         teristics of an ideal observer and everything else were
         the same.

According to (III), the truth of moral judgments is relative to
particular individuals. As I argued in Chapter Two, it is most likely
that there are at least some moral questions concerning which all
human ideal observers would have the same attitudes, so (III) is
compatible with the view that there are some moral judgments
that are correct for all human beings. Even though (III) implies
that there are many moral issues concerning which there are judgments that are at most true for certain individuals, it still implies
that such judgments are correct in a sense that is opposed to
incorrect. In this sense of 'correct' if it is correct for someone
to hold a particular moral judgment then it would be incorrect
for him to hold any conflicting judgment instead. I will argue that
this view, according to which judgments about many moral issues
can be correct only in the very weak sense of being correct for
particular individuals, still permits us to make moral judgments.

However, the sorts of moral judgments that my view permits in cases in which there is no judgment that is correct for all human beings cannot serve all of the same functions as our ordinary moral judgments. Some of those functions presuppose that moral judgments are correct at least in the sense of being correct for all human beings.

I want to consider the question of whether or not it is consistent for me to make moral judgments about questions concerning which I believe that there is no judgment that is true for all human beings in the context of the larger issue of the connection between first-order moral judgments and meta-ethical views about the status of moral judgments. Before arguing that my own version of ethical relativism permits us to make moral judgments, I will argue that those versions of meta-ethical relativism that imply that it is impossible for a person's moral judgments to be mistaken are nihilistic views in the sense that it is inconsistent for those who hold such views to make any moral judgments.[1] Many standard versions of ethical relativism, e.g., the view that whatever moral judgments a person accepts are true for him, rule out the possibility that a person's moral judgments could be mistaken and therefore constitute a kind of nihilism.

Chapter Four extends the discussion begun here. I will consider the connection between meta-ethical views and first-order attitudes and emotions and attempt to determine whether or not any commonplace attitudes or emotions presuppose a belief in the objectivity of morals.

3.1. SOME DIFFERENT MEANINGS OF THE TERM 'ETHICAL RELATIVISM'

Before turning to the main argument of this chapter, I would first like to define 'meta-ethical relativism' and distinguish it from other versions of moral relativism.

3.1.1. Cultural Relativism

It is often claimed that morality is 'relative'. The claim that morality is relative typically involves the denial that it is 'absolute', 'universal', or 'objective'. But this does not make clear everything that is meant when it is said that morality is relative. What is meant by 'morality' and what is it that morality is supposed to be relative *to*? The terms 'morals' and 'morality' are sometimes used to refer to the standards or beliefs about moral questions that are accepted by particular groups or individuals. For example, to say that someone's activities are incompatible with society's morals is to say that those acts are contrary to the society's conventional moral standards. To say that morality (in this sense of the term) is relative is to say that beliefs or opinions about moral issues are relative to different individuals and different societies, i.e., different individuals and different societies accept different moral standards and hold incompatible views about many moral questions. This view is often labeled "cultural" or "sociological" relativism. Cultural relativism is an empirical view and as stated it is clearly true: there are few, if any, moral issues concerning which everyone agrees. There is, however, some controversy over the question of whether disagreements between different individuals and different societies reflect any disagreement over ultimate moral principles. The fact that two people disagree as to the rightness of wrongness of a particular act does not show that they disagree at the level of basic moral principles – they may simply disagree about certain factual questions concerning the nature of the act, for instance, whether or not it is likely to cause anyone great suffering.[2]

3.1.2. Situational Relativism

Many people hold that the moral status of an action or state of affairs is relative to the situation in which it occurs or is performed. (I will call this view 'situational relativism'.) For instance, most people would say that whether or not it is morally permissible to tell a lie is relative to the situation in which the lie is told. Lying is permissible in some situations, for example, when it is necessary in order to save the life of an innocent person, and wrong in other situations. Or, to take another example that few would deny, it is obligatory to drive on the right side of the road in the United States and obligatory to drive on the left side of the road in Great Britain. Almost all moral philosophers would accept some version or other of situational relativism.[3] The kinds of considerations that lead people to accept situational relativism are sometimes taken to support the view that there are no moral "absolutes". The rejection of moral absolutes in this context amounts to the view that there is nothing that is always good or always bad and nothing that is always right or always wrong and thus, that there are no general moral principles that hold true without exception in all circumstances. But this conclusion does not follow. The mere fact that lying is neither wrong in all circumstances nor permissible in all circumstances does not show that there are no valid general principles about lying. For 'lying is always wrong' and 'lying is always permissible' are not the only possible principles about lying. Some alternative general principles about the moral status of lying that are more plausible than either of these are the following: 'lying is permissible if and only if it results in better consequences than not lying' and 'lying is permissible if and only if it is necessary in order to avoid very bad consequences or fulfill some other important obligation such as keeping a promise'. Perhaps there are exceptions to these principles as well. However, that would not suggest that there are no correct general principles about the moral status of lying, but only that such principles must involve very elaborate and specific descriptions of classes of actions (much more careful

descriptions than it is worth worrying about for ordinary purposes).

3.1.3. Normative Relativism

It is often asserted that it is a mistake to judge another person
by one's own moral standards or the standards of one's own
society; we should judge other people and what they do by reference to their own moral standards or the standards of the
societies of which they are members. According to this view,
which Brandt and Frankena call "normative relativism", the
moral status of a person and what he does is relative to his own
moral standards or the standards of the society of which he is a
member.[4] There are a number of different ways in which normative relativism can be formulated, for example:

> An act is right iff the agent believes that it is right.

> An act is right iff it is consistent with the basic moral
> principles of the agent or the basic moral principles of
> the society of which the agent is a member.

> An individual is a good person iff he believes that he is
> good.

It is no doubt very important to consider the principles of the
agent and the agent's society when making moral judgments about
his conduct. We need to know what sorts of principles a person
accepts in order to know whether or not he acts conscientiously
and, at the very least, an agent possesses some moral worth in
virtue of being consceientious. Moral observers also need to be
aware of the customs and conventions of the agent's society,
because the effects of the agent's acts and his understanding of
his actions is determined largely by convention. For example,
whether or not conduct should be interpreted as respectful or

disrespectful is almost entirely a matter of convention. These considerations, however, are not enough to support normative relativism; they could be fully accepted by people holding incompatible views. Not only are the usual reasons put forward in favor of normative relativism inadequate, there are reasons for thinking that it is a very implausible view. Normative relativism has a number of consequences that are extremely counter-intuitive. Among other things it implies that a person can be justified in doing *anything* whatever, including acts of murder and torture etc., provided that his doing so is consistent with his own basic moral standards or the basic standards of the society of which he is a member.

3.1.4. Meta-Ethical Relativism

In the philosophical literature ethical relativism is usually defined as the view that conflicting moral judgments can be equally correct or equally valid. To say that conflicting judgments can be equally valid means that several different people may each be correct in holding conflicting views about certain moral questions. For example it may be correct for me to hold that a certain act is morally permissible and equally correct for you to think that that same act is morally wrong. According to this view, which is usually called "meta-ethical relativism", the *truth* or *correctness* of moral judgments is relative to the standards of different individuals or different societies and there are no valid ways of arbitrating between incompatible moral standards. Meta-ethical relativism is the version of ethical relativism that is associated with the familiar 'true for you', 'true for me' terminology. Meta-ethical relativism is a view about the *status* of moral judgments. It implies that moral judgments are not objectively true or false but only true or false *for* particular individuals or particular groups. Normative relativism, on the other hand, is a substantive or first-order moral theory and does not entail any particular view about the status of moral judgments. Normative relativism is quite compatible with the view that moral judgments are objectively correct. It would be consistent for a normative relativist to say that it's objectively true that a person should always do whatever is required by his own basic moral principles.

3.1.5. *Meta-Ethical Relativism Contrasted with Moral Skepticism*

Metal-ethical relativism should not be confused with moral skepticism. A moral skeptic is someone who denies that people have or can have knowledge about moral questions. For example, a moral skeptic might say that it is impossible to know whether or not it would be right for Mrs. Jones to have an abortion. The skeptic, however, can still say that there is an objectively correct view concerning this and other moral issues. There is no reason why the skeptic can't say that it *may* be objectively correct to think that it would be permissible for Mrs. Jones to have an abortion. All that he needs to deny is that anyone could ever *know* this. (Similarly, it is consistent for the person who thinks that it is impossible to know whether or not the first forms of life on earth lived in fresh water to think that it is either objectively true or false that the first forms of life lived in fresh water.) Meta-ethical relativism is a much more radical view than moral skepticism. The meta-ethical relativist not only says that we cannot *know* whether things are good or bad or right or wrong, etc., he denies that there are any moral truths (any objectively correct views about moral questions) for us to know.

3.2. THE DEFINITION OF 'META-ETHICAL RELATIVISM'

3.2.1. *An Objection to the Standard Definition*

As was noted earlier, the term 'ethical relativism' (or 'meta-ethical relativism') is usually defined as the view that conflicting ethical judgments can be equally correct or equally valid. In *Ethical Theory*, Richard Brandt defines ethical relativism as the view that *"There are conflicting ethical opinions that are equally valid"*.[5] Paul Taylor defines ethical relativism as "the assertion that two or more people or groups of people may hold contradictory ethical views without either being mistaken".[6] Gilbert Harman says that "according to meta-ethical relativism, there can be conflicting moral judgments about a particular case that are both fully correct".[7] There are a great many other philosophers who define ethical relativism or meta-ethical relativism along these same lines.[8]

There are serious difficulties with the standard definition of meta-ethical relativism. For even the most thorough-going absolutist would be prepared to say that sometimes two moral judgments can be equally absurd and thus also equally correct (or incorrect if you prefer). Consider the following judgments:

(i)   All Icelanders ought to be boiled to death.
(ii)   All Icelanders ought to be broiled to death.

An absolutist and a relativist could both agree that (i) and (ii) are equally correct (or incorrect). The absolutist, however, can consistently hold that there is a third conflicting judgment, e.g., 'it's not the case that all Icelanders ought to be killed', that is more correct than all other conflicting judgments, and this is precisely what distinguishes his view from the relativist's.

3.2.2. A Revised Definition

In order to avoid the implication that one would be a meta-ethical relativist simply in virtue of holding that (i) and (ii) are equally correct I suggest the following revised definition of meta-ethical relativism:

(A)   Meta-ethical relativism is the view that there are moral
        issues about which there is no moral judgment that is
        more correct than all other conflicting judgments.

The standard definition of 'meta-ethical relativism', which I have
refined but not abandoned, employs the concept of a judgment's
being 'more correct' than another. It might be objected that this
concept implies that correctness is a property of all judgments,
which admits of many different degrees. Perhaps there is no
common scalar property of correctness shared to varying degrees
by all judgments. Perhaps a false or incorrect judgment isn't
correct to a lesser degree than a true judgment; it might be more
accurate to say that it simply isn't correct at all. I suspect that
many relativists would claim that correctness is a special property
of all judgments and that it admits of many different degrees.
However, I do not want the intelligibility of the standard definition of meta-ethical relativism to depend on this dubious assumption. So, let me suggest, or rather stipulate, a way of interpreting
the expressions 'x is more correct than y' and 'x and y are equally
correct' that doesn't presuppose that correctness is a kind of
scalar property similar to heat or mass. Suppose that we say that
moral judgments must be either correct or incorrect – period –
just as a factual statement must be either true or false. We can
still use the concepts of a correct and incorrect judgment to define
the following notions:

(1)   A correct moral judgment is *more correct* than an
        incorrect judgment.
(2)   Two correct judgments are *equally correct*.
(3)   Two incorrect judgments are *equally correct*.

We can give sense to the idea that judgments can admit of many
different degrees of correctness in the following way:

A judgment is correct to the degree that it approaches the truth.

x is more correct than y if, and only if, x is closer to the truth than y.

x and y are equally correct if, and only if, they are equally close to the truth.

I shall not attempt to offer a precise analysis of the concept of one judgment's 'being closer to the truth' than another or the concept of two judgments being 'equally close to the truth'. However, the legitimacy of these two concepts can be seen from the following two examples. Suppose that I say that the earth is one mile from the sun and you say that the earth is 90 million miles from the sun. Both statements are false. However, yours is 'closer to the truth' than mine and therefore 'more correct'. Suppose, on the other hand, that you say that the earth is 90 million miles from the sun and I say that it is 96 million miles away. Both statements are equally close to the truth and, therefore, in the sense that we have defined, 'equally correct'.

When relativists say that there are conflicting moral judgments that are equally valid, they typically mean that conflicting judgments can be *valid for different individuals*. In other words, two different individuals can accept conflicting judgments without either of them being mistaken. Some relativists also hold that conflicting moral judgments can be equally correct *for particular individuals*, i.e., a person may be such that it would be equally correct for him to accept either of two conflicting judgments (even if there is no third judgment that it would be more correct for him to accept). For our purposes here I will take (A) to mean that there are moral issues concerning which conflicting judgments can be equally valid for *different individuals*. (A) does not necessarily imply that there are any moral issues concerning which it would be equally correct for *a particular individual* to accept either one of two conflicting judgments (without it also being the case that there is some third judgment that it would be more correct for him to accept than either of the first two judgments).

3.2.3. *Some Derivative Notions*

Using (A) we can also define the following notions:

(B)   Moderate meta-ethical relativism is the view that some, but not all, moral issues are such that there is no moral judgment concerning them that is more correct than all other conflicting judgments.

(C)   Extreme meta-ethical relativism is the view that no moral issues are such that there is a moral judgment concerning them that is more correct than all other conflicting judgments.

Note that extreme relativism differs from the following view:

(D)   All conflicting moral judgments are equally correct, i.e., there is no pair of conflicting moral judgments that is such that one can be said to be more correct than the other.

Extreme relativism implies that whenever one makes a moral judgment *at least one* of the judgments that conflicts with it is at least as correct as it is. (D), which is a much more extreme principle, implies that whenever one makes a moral judgment *all* of the judgments that conflict with it are at least as correct as it is. (C) allows for the possibility of rational criticism of moral judgments. It allows for the possibility that a person's judgments are not as correct as certain other judgments that he might have accepted instead. The following example may serve to illustrate the difference between (C) and (D). A person who accepts (C) might say that the view that capital punishment is justified only for first-degree murder is just as correct as the view that it is never justified and that both views are more correct than the view that capital punishment can be justified for any crime, including petty theft. The person who accepts (D), however, must say that all of these views are equally correct.

3.3. SOME NECESSARY CONDITIONS OF ONE'S ACCEPTING A MORAL JUDGMENT OR A MORAL PRINCIPLE

My arguments to show that several standard versions of meta-ethical relativism are nihilistic views depend on the following assumptions:

(1)   A necessary condition of one's holding or accepting a moral judgment is that one think that it would be a mistake or an error for one to accept any conflicting judgment. (This does not simply mean that if one accepts a moral judgment, j, then one must believe that it would be a mistake for one to accept both j and some conflicting judgment, not-j, rather it means that a necessary condition of one's accepting j is that one think that it would be a mistake for one to accept not-j instead of j.)[9]

(2)   A necessary condition of one's accepting something *as a moral principle* is that one think that it would be a mistake or an error for one to accept any conflicting principle.

I shall attempt to defend these two principles here.

3.3.1. A Moral Judgment

A necessary condition of one's believing that x is that one think that it would be a mistake for one to accept any conflicting proposition instead of x, otherwise one would have no reason to accept x as opposed to the other proposition. This does not just amount to saying that a necessary condition of one's *believing that x is objectively true* is that one think that it would be a mistake for one to believe anything that conflicts with x. Even if I just believe that x is 'true for me', I must believe that it would be a mistake for me to believe anything that conflicts with x, (c), because otherwise I could not be said to believe x *rather than c*. It is incoherent to say 'I believe that it's true for me that x and not c, however, it would be equally correct for me to believe that c and not x instead'.

It might be argued that cases in which a person believes something that he takes to be no more well supported by the evidence than conflicting views constitute counter-examples to (1). I can believe that x, even if I think that there is equal or even greater evidence for some conflicting proposition. Such cases, however, are not counter-examples to (1). For to say that a belief is *well-supported by the available evidence* is not the same as saying that it is *correct*. A theist might concede that his beliefs are no more reasonable or well-supported by the evidence than those of an atheist. But the theist does not say that it would be equally correct for him to believe that God does not exist. On his view this belief would be *mistaken* because God actually does exist. (Think of Tertullian.)

3.3.2. A Moral Principle

A necessary condition of one's accepting something *as a moral principle* is that one think that it would be a mistake for one to accept any conflicting principle — otherwise one could not be said to accept that particular principle as opposed to another. To accept a princple is to reject conflicting or incompatible principles (at least when one is aware of their incompatibility). If one accepts a principle, p, one must have some reason (where 'reason' is construed in the sense of motivation, not in the sense of evidence or justification) for accepting that particular principle as opposed to some alternative principle. It is incoherent to say such things as 'One should always act so as to bring about the best possible consequences; however, there are certain non-utilitarian principles that it would be equally correct for one to accept instead'.

It might be objected that a person can be motivated to adopt one moral principle as opposed to another, even if he does not think that it is correct (in a sense that is opposed to incorrect) for him to adopt any particular principle. One may choose one principle over another simply as a matter of whim or because one prefers to follow the one rather than the other. It is indeed true that one can adopt and follow *practical principles* simply as a matter of whim or preference or for any reason whatever. Nevertheless, a necessary condition of one's *adopting something as a moral principle* is that one believe that it is correct (in a sense that is opposed to incorrect) for one to adopt that principle. This can best be seen by considering examples of principles that are *accepted as moral principles* by some people and *accepted but not accepted as moral principles* by others. Any moral principle can be adopted or followed by someone without it being the case that he accepts it as a moral principle. A person who follows and avows an absolute prohibition against killing simply as a matter of whim cannot be said to believe that killing is morally wrong.

Consider the case of a man who is very averse to homosexuality. Not only is he disgusted at the thought of *his* being a homosexual,

he is disgusted by other people who are homosexuals. He follows
the principle 'avoid all homosexual acts' and encourages others
to do so as well. Clearly this description is consistent with its
being the case that he does not think that there is anything
morally wrong with homosexuality. (This is a good example
because there are many people who have very unfavorable attitudes about homosexuality without thinking that it is morally
wrong.) The difference between him and someone who "really"
thinks that homosexuality is wrong is that the latter not only
has an aversion to homosexuality (he does not even have to have
such an aversion, for many people who have strong homosexual
tendencies believe that homosexuality is wrong), he also thinks
that it is correct or appropriate for him to have such an aversion.
He thinks that it would be incorrect for him to approve of homosexuality, even if his preferences were of a very different sort and
he had no particular aversion to it. On the other hand, if one's
practical commitments against homosexuality are based simply
on preferences that one does not take to be correct (if one does
not think that it would be incorrect for one to like or approve
of homosexuality) then one cannot be said to believe that homosexuality is morally wrong. I think that (2) is part of what accounts for the fact that we believe that moral considerations
place *demands* upon us that are independent of our will.[10] If I
adopt a practical principle simply as a matter of whim then I
cannot be said to feel that it places any demands on me, since I
am always free to reject it. The same considerations also count
in favor of (1).

3.4. META-ETHICAL RELATIVISM AND NIHILISM

I shall now argue that it is inconsistent for individuals who accept
those versions of meta-ethical relativism according to which a

person's moral judgments cannot possibly be mistaken to make any moral judgments.

3.4.1. A Preliminary Argument

Extreme meta-ethical relativism implies that, for any moral judgment, there is at least one conflicting judgment that is equally correct. Suppose that an extreme meta-ethical relativist attempts to make a moral judgment. For instance, he might say that incest is never morally permissible. The relativist, however, must be prepared to say in the same breath that there is at least one conflicting opinion, e.g., 'incest is sometimes morally permissible' that is equally correct. This is giving with one hand and taking away with the other. To add the proviso that there is a conflicting judgment that is equally correct is to cancel out the original judgment. It is as if one were to say 'I'm going but I'm not going' or 'shut the door but don't shut it'.

It is part of the logic or meaning of moral judgments (and other sorts of judgments as well) to imply that all conflicting judgments are in some sense less valid.[11] Imagine that I wish to issue a moral condemnation of the Nazi "final solution". My judgment must be taken to imply that my own views and attitudes about the final solution are more correct than those of people who approve of it. To condemn the final solution is, at the very least, to reject the views of an ardent Nazi. To reject someone's views, as opposed to merely making a statement to the effect that one's own views are different, is to impugn the correctness of the other person's views.

The same kind of argument can be given to show that a moderate meta-ethical relativist cannot make moral judgments about any of those issues concerning which he believes that there is no correct position. Suppose that I believe that there are no correct views about the moral status of abortion. In that case, I cannot make any moral judgments about abortion because, for any moral judgment about abortion which I may wish to make, e.g., 'abortion is permissible when it is necessary in order to save the life of the mother', I must be prepared to say that it would be equally correct to deny this.

3.4.2. An Objection Considered

At this point the relativist may wish to offer the following reply: "I concede that my position involves a denial of the objective truth or correctness of moral judgments. I also concede that moral judgments involve the assertion of their own correctness. I cannot make a moral judgment if I am prepared to admit that conflicting judgments are equally correct or valid. I must be prepared to say that my own judgments are more correct than all conflicting judgments. However, I needn't claim that my judgments are objectively true or true for all human beings. In order to make moral judgments, I only need to claim that my judgments are true (correct) *for me* and that conflicting judgments are less true (correct) *for me*."

3.4.3. The Concept of Subjective Truth

We must ask what it means to say that a moral judgment is 'true for' a particular individual. A moral judgment's being true for someone is not the same as its being objectively true or true in the ordinary sense. If a moral judgment or moral principle is true in the ordinary sense, then it must be true for everyone or correct for everyone to accept it. However, to say that something is true *for me* is to suggest that it may be false for someone else.

As many people use the notion of subjective truth, to say that a judgment is true for someone is simply to say that he believes it. Some relativists hold that moral judgments are true or correct only in the above sense. I shall call this view R1. According to R1, a person's views about moral questions can never be mistaken because any moral judgment that a person accepts is true for him.[12] R1 cannot save the relativist from nihilism. For if a moral judgment's being true for someone consists in nothing more than his believing it, then a moral judgment could be true for someone, even if it would be equally correct for him to accept some conflicting judgment instead. R1 is subject to precisely the same problem noted earlier: if I accept R1 and try to make a moral judgment, e.g., 'it's true for me that _____', I must be prepared to say that it would be equally correct for me to accept *any* other conflicting judgment instead, thus effectively cancelling out the original judgment. The argument can be put more generally as follows: a person who accepts R1 cannot believe or accept any moral judgments, without being inconsistent. In order for one to believe or accept a moral judgment it is necessary that one think that it would be a mistake for one to accept any conflicting judgment. However, if one accepts R1, then one can never say that it would be a mistake for one to accept one moral judgment rather than another.

3.5. A NON-NIHILISTIC VERSION OF META-ETHICAL RELATIVISM

3.5.1. *Two Necessary Conditions for a Non-Nihilistic Version of Meta-Ethical Relativism*

Any view according to which a person's sincerely held moral judgments cannot possibly be mistaken or according to which they are not subject to rational criticism constitutes a nihilistic view. In order to avoid nihilism the relativist needs to develop a concept of subjective truth that allows for the possibility that a person accepts judgments that it is incorrect for him to hold.

Only when it is admitted that there are judgments that it would be incorrect for one to hold (in fact only when it is admitted that it would be incorrect for one to hold any judgments that are inconsistent with those that it is correct for one to hold) can one make moral judgments without being prepared at the same time to add the nullifying proviso that it would be equally correct for one to accept some conflicting judgment.

What kind of notion of subjective truth is required in order for the relativist to avoid nihilism? At the very least, the relativist's notion of correctness must be one that is opposed to incorrectness. To say that it is correct for S to accept a moral judgment must be taken to imply that it would be incorrect for him to accept any conflicting judgment instead. In order to avoid nihilism, the relativist must say that moral judgments are correct in this sense — their being correct for someone means that it would be incorrect for him to accept any conflicting judgment. In order to be a relativist, however, he must hold that moral judgments are not objectively correct. The fact that it is correct for one person to hold a particular moral judgment does not mean that it would be correct for everyone else to accept that same judgment. For example, a relativist might say that it is true for him that it could never be morally right for someone to have an abortion. In order for this to constitute a moral judgment, he must be prepared to say that it would be incorrect for him to hold any judgment that conflicts with this. However, inasmuch as he is a relativist, he cannot say that his judgment is objectively correct — he must grant that there are, or could be, people who are such that it would be incorrect for them to think that having an abortion is never morally permissible.

3.5.2. *That the View Defended in Chapter Two Constitutes a Non-Nihilistic Version of Meta-Ethical Relativism*

In Chapter Two I suggested the following principle as a criterion for the correctness of an individual person's moral judgments:

(III)   It is correct (in a sense that is opposed to mistaken) for S to accept a favorable (unfavorable) moral judgment about x if, and only if, S would have a favorable (unfavorable) attitude about x if he possessed all of the essential features of an ideal observer.

(III) can be reformulated as a 'judgment version' of the IOT as follows:

(III′)   It is correct (in a sense that is opposed to mistaken) for S to accept a moral judgment, j, if, and only if, S would accept j if he had all of the essential features of an ideal observer.

(III) and (III′) satisfy our two conditions for being non-nihilistic versions of meta-ethical relativism. (1) They imply that moral judgments can be correct in a sense that is opposed to incorrect and that it is possible for a person's moral judgments to be mistaken. For example, they imply, that if it is the case that I would strongly disapprove of Hitler if I were an ideal observer, then my judgment that he was a good man is mistaken. (2) (III) and (III′) allow for the possibility that it could be correct for different people to hold conflicting judgments about certain moral questions. If two people would continue to hold opposed attitudes about questions concerning abortion even if they were to become ideal observers, then it follows that it is correct for them to hold conflicting views about this issue.

3.5.3. Other Non-Nihilistic Versions of Meta-Ethical Relativism

There are conceivably other non-nihilistic versions of meta-ethical relativism. One view that might seem to fit this description is the following:

> For any person, *S*, and moral judgment, *j*, concerning *x*, *j* is true for *S* iff *S*'s basic moral principles taken together with the set of true factual statements that describe *x* entail *j*.

The view that moral judgments are true or correct only in this sense I will call (IV).[13] (IV) appears to satisfy the two conditions for being a non-nihilistic version of relativism. (1) It allows for the possibility that a particular moral judgment could be true for one individual or one group of people but not another (if the two individuals or two groups have incompatible basic moral principles). (2) It implies that if a moral judgment is true for someone, then it would be incorrect for him to accept any moral judgment that conflicts with it — *so long as his basic principles remain the same.*

Nevertheless, (IV) is a nihilistic view. It implies that any judgment that is consistent with one's basic moral principles is true for one and thus that one's moral judgments cannot be criticized, provided that they are entailed by the conjunction of one's basic moral principles and the set of all true factual statements. (IV) also seems to commit one to the view that the choice of basic moral principles is arbitrary — at least from the standpoint of concern for the truth. A person who is concerned only that his principles be true rather than false cannot have any reason to accept any particular moral principle, as opposed to other alternative principles. (According to (IV), the standard of correctness for moral judgments is simply one's basic moral principles — whatever they happen to be; for a moral judgment to be true or correct

for one is simply for it to be in accordance with one's principles.)
If (IV) is true, then it cannot be correct (in a sense that is opposed
to incorrect) to choose one set of moral principles over all of the
other alternative principles, because any set of principles will yield
correct moral judgments if it is appropriately adhered to.[14]

If (IV) is true, then no moral judgments can be true for someone unless he accepts at least one first-order moral principle — if
he does not accept any such principles, then no moral judgments
can be true for him. There cannot be any moral judgments that
follow from the conjunction of true factual statements and one's
basic moral principles, unless one accepts some moral principles.
As we have seen earlier, in order for one to accept one moral principle as opposed to another it is necessary that one view the acceptance of the one over the other as somehow appropriate or correct
in a sense that is opposed to inappropriate or incorrect. One cannot be said to accept something as a moral principle if one thinks
that it would be equally correct for one to accept some incompatible principle. But, as we have seen, (IV) implies that it can
never be more correct for one to accept a particular principle
rather than all of the other principles that one might have accepted instead. If the proponent of (IV) is consistent and accepts
no first-order moral principles, then (IV) implies that no moral
judgments can be true for him. This means that, according to his
own principles, any moral judgments that he might make would
be mistaken. One who accepts (IV), however, can still say that
moral judgments are *true for others*. Others can accept moral
principles in the way required, but only if they accept incorrect
meta-ethical theories or are inconsistent. According to (IV) there
being moral judgments that are true for others is ultimately dependent on their having made some kind of error.

Consider the following:

(V)   A moral judgment is true for S iff it is entailed by the conjunction of the basic moral principles of S's society and some set of true factual statements.[15]

(V) satisfies the two conditions set down earlier. (1) It allows for the possibility that one's moral judgments can be mistaken — according to (V) one's moral judgments are mistaken unless they follow from the conjunction of the basic moral principles of one's society and some set of true factual statements. (2) (V) implies that it can be correct for two different individuals to accept conflicting moral judgments, provided that they are members of societies that have incompatible basic moral principles. While (V) is a *bona fide* non-nihilistic version of meta-ethical relativism, there do not seem to be any good reasons for thinking that it is true or correct. I know of no reason to suppose that it is incorrect to accept moral judgments that are inconsistent with the principles of one's society.

3.6. CONCLUSION

3.6.1. *My Theory Is Not a Rejection of Morality in Toto*

As I argued in Chapter One (Section 1.2.10), many of the characteristic functions of moral judgments require that they be generally assumed to be objectively true or at least true for all human beings. Moral judgments could not serve the functions of prescribing actions to other people and influencing their attitudes unless they purported to be correct for all human beings. They could not perform these functions if most people were to come to accept my view about the status of moral judgments. My view denies much of what is implicit in our ordinary moral notions. Nevertheless, it is compatible with morality in some more limited sense. My view permits us to assess the correctness of our own attitudes and those of others. It also permits us to make moral judgments about our own conduct and that of others; judgments about what other people do can be prescriptive only when those judgments are correct for all human beings.

My view commits us to abandoning certain assumptions about the nature of moral disagreement. In ordinary circumstances, if two people have conflicting views about a moral question, we say that they *disagree* about it. If they discover that they hold conflicting views, they are not content to let the disagreement persist — each will attempt to persuade the other to adopt his position or they may call their own views into question. The tendency to do this depends on the shared supposition that moral judgments are objectively correct or at least correct for all human beings. If two people hold conflicting moral judgments, it is assumed that at least one of them must be mistaken, because at least one of them must hold a view that is inconsistent with the objectively correct view or the view that is correct for all human beings. Given the objectivity of morals, if one's own views are correct, then all conflicting views must be mistaken. If my version of relativism is true, however, the fact that one's own views are correct does not imply that those who have conflicting views are mistaken. The relativist need not have any special concern to resolve conflicts of opinion about moral issues. For, on his view, people can hold conflicting views about certain moral questions without any of them being in error. (It is just this tolerance for conflict that makes relativism so attractive to many people.) In fact, the relativist may find himself in the peculiar position of trying to persuade others to adopt moral judgments that are inconsistent with those that he accepts. Suppose that a relativist and his friend both agree that abortion is always wrong. The relativist presumably believes that it is correct for him to think that abortion is always wrong. However, he may also believe that it is incorrect for his friend to think that abortion is always wrong. In that case he may attempt to persuade his friend to adopt views incompatible with his own simply in order that his friend have correct views. If two relativists have conflicting views about some issue, then they have incompatible attitudes about it and the attitude that the one believes it correct for him to have is incompatible with the attitude which the other thinks it correct for *him* to have. But the mere fact that they have conflicting views about some issue does not imply that either thinks that the other is mistaken or that either has any desire to persuade the other to alter his views.

3.6.2. An Objection Considered

Let me conclude this chapter by considering a possible objection to my contention that the view defended at the end of Chapter Two (III) constitutes a non-nihilistic version of ethical relativism, i.e., a view that permits us to make moral judgments even about those issues concerning which there is no judgment that is correct for all human beings. B. C. Postow argues that relativists cannot consistently make moral judgments about the conduct of others.[16] If correct, her arguments also apply to my position. Her argument can be stated as follows. If (III) is true, then we should expect there to be cases of the following sort. It is true for me that S ought to do x and true for S that he has no obligation to do x. But if it is true for S that he has no obligation to do x, then he cannot have a moral reason, all things considered, to do it. For to say that someone is obligated to do something is to imply that he has moral reasons, all things considered, to do it. According to Postow, it would be dishonest for me to tell S that he ought to do x because I know that he has no moral reason to do x all things considered. Postow is assuming that whether or not a person has moral reasons to do something (all things considered) is a matter of objective fact. But no relativist would grant her this assumption. It would be perfectly in order for the relativist to say 'It's true for *me* that S has reasons to do x and false for S that he has reasons to do x'.

There are two objections that might be offered here. (1) It could be argued that the possibility that I am arguing for is ruled out by reflection on the notion of what it is for someone to have reasons for action. If S has reasons for doing x, then these reasons must be capable of motivating him to do x in the appropriate circumstances. If S has reasons for doing x, all things considered, then it must be the case that he would do it if he were informed or fully cognizant of these reasons. Therefore, it cannot be true for me that S has reasons to do x unless it is also true for him that he has reasons to do x. (2) Another objection is that to say that S's doing x is wrong entails that S made a mistake in choosing to do x rather than something else. It doesn't make any sense to say that someone did something wrong unless his decision to do it can be faulted.

With some trepidation I offer the following replies. (a) The first objection presupposes that someone's having reasons to do x means or entails roughly 'S would be motivated to x under ideal circumstances'. But this assumption is dubious. The following account of reasons for action is open to the relativist: 'It is true for ＿＿＿ that S ought to do x iff ＿＿＿ would choose or prefer that S do x if he were fully informed, etc.' We are talking about what it is for S to have reasons to do x and it no doubt seems implausible to analyze this in terms of what ＿＿＿ (who is most likely not identical with S) would do in that situation. However, we are not analyzing what it is for it to be objectively true that S has reasons to do x; we are analyzing what it is for it to be true for ＿＿＿ that S has reasons to do x. To assume that reasons for S to do x must be capable of motivating *him* is simply to beg the question. (b) Ordinarily, the claim that someone did something wrong can be taken to imply that his decision to do the act in question can be faulted. 'It is objectively true that it was wrong for S to do x' entails 'it is objectively true that S's decision to do x can be faulted' (i.e., it would be correct in a sense that is opposed to mistaken for anyone to fault S's decision). Similarly, 'it is objectively true that it was right for S to do x' entails 'it is objectively true that S's decision to do x can't be faulted'. However, *it is true for S* that his doing x is right' only entails 'it is true for S that his decision to do x rather than something else can't be faulted', i.e., it is correct for him not to disapprove of his decision. It does not entail that it is true for me that his decision to do x can't be faulted. Its being appropriate for S to approve of his decision to do x leaves open the possibility that it is appropriate for others to disapprove of it.

If Postow's arguments prevail against these replies, then contrary to what I have argued here, the position defended in Chapters One and Two comes close to being a complete rejection of morality. (In that case, my position would still fall short of being a total rejection of morality, since there are presumably some moral issues concerning which there is a judgment that is true for all human beings.) Even if my replies to her arguments succeed, her arguments would seem to show that, on my view, moral judgments about the rightness or wrongness of other people's conduct cannot have prescriptive force. My judgment that it is wrong for you to do x can't effectively prescribe that you not do x because it leaves open the possibility that it would be perfectly correct for you not to disapprove of your doing x. Similarly, its being true for someone else that your doing something is permissible does not entail that it would be correct for you to approve of your decision to do it. This conclusion, that my version of relativism implies that moral judgments about the conduct of other people cannot be prescriptive, is one that we reached earlier on independent grounds — see Section 1.2.10. Assuming that there are very few moral issues concerning which all ideal observers would share the same attitudes, the views

defended in Chapter Two constitute a rejection of much of what
is implicit in our ordinary moral judgments. However, my position
is compatible with a system of practical reasoning that has many
of the features of our ordinary moral judgments.

THE WAGES OF RELATIVISM

Philosophers have traditionally considered questions about the status of norms to be of great significance. Most have thought that it matters very much whether or not our normative judgments can be said to be true or correct. Much of the writing of the existentialist philosophers is given to an examination of what are perceived to be the momentous consequences of our loss of grounds for belief in the objectivity of moral and other sorts of normative standards. Renouncing belief in the objectivity of morals is thought to compel one to abandon certain kinds of fundamental attitudes and commitments. It might seem that the results arrived at in this book compel me to make such a renunciation. In this chapter I shall endeavor to determine whether any of the usual attitudes and commitments of ordinary human beings presuppose any particular views about the status of norms. More specifically, I will atempt to determine whether any ordinary human commitments or attitudes about the world are inconsistent with either: (1) the view that normative judgments are not correct in any sense that is opposed to mistaken (I will call this view 'hard meta-ethical relativism' or 'HMER') − HMER is equivalent to what I called "nihilistic relativism" in Chapter Three (I am dropping this terminology here, since it tends to prejudge the issues to be considered in this chapter); or (2) 'soft meta-ethical relativism' ('SMER') − the view that normative judgments are not objectively correct or correct for all rational beings, but are still correct in some sense that is opposed to mistaken. The position defended in Chapter Two is a version of SMER. The primary difference between HMER and SMER is that SMER permits one to make judgments to the effect that it is correct (in a sense that is opposed to mistaken) for a certain individual to accept a particular moral judgment while HMER does not permit one to say this.

I shall argue that the character of our first-order attitudes is, in many cases, causally dependent on our views as to the status of norms. The abandonment of objectivist views may bring about very profound changes in certain sorts of individuals. There are also certain types of people whose first-order attitudes are relatively independent of their meta-ethical views. Logical or conceptual connections between first-order attitudes and meta-ethical views are much more difficult to discern. Most attitudes about the world and things in the world are logically compatible with any kind of meta-ethical view. However, I will argue that such attitudes as guilt and resentment presuppose a belief in the falsity of HMER.

4.1. WHAT SORTS OF ATTITUDES AND COMMITMENTS PRESUPPOSE A BELIEF IN THE OBJECTIVITY OF NORMATIVE JUDGMENTS?

4.1.1. Normative Judgments Are Statements About the Correctness of Attitudes

As we saw in Chapter One, there is an intimate connection between attitudes and norms. Normative considerations can either justify or discredit attitudes. For example, to say that x is good (or that it is objectively true that x is good) is to imply that it is correct or appropriate for any rational being to have a favorable attitude about x. To say that something is intrinsically bad is to say that it is correct to have an unfavorable attitude about it. Attitudes concerning something cannot be said to be objectively correct unless there are objectively correct normative judgments

about it. Any facts about the world that would make certain
attitudes objectively correct are *ipso facto* moral facts or normative facts.

4.1.2. *HMER Does Not Commit One to Being Indifferent to Everything*

Most people have strong desires and preferences with respect to
a great many different things. For example, I have a strong desire
for my continued existence and the continued existence of a
great many other people. Some have thought that the abandonment of any belief in the objectivity or correctness of one's own
normative judgments commits one to abandoning all of one's
desires and preferences, i.e., being the sort of person who does't
care about anything, the sort of person for whom nothing matters.
The argument is that one cannot have any reason to choose or
prefer one thing to another, since one has no reason to think
that it is true in any significant sense that one thing is better
than another. For any judgment that I make to the effect that
x is better than y, I must be prepared to say that it would be
equally correct for me to say that y is better than x.

Before considering this argument it would be well to determine
what would be required for being completely indifferent to everything and to consider some possible examples of such indifference.
It is unlikely that there has ever been a person who was totally
indifferent to *everything* throughout any significant period of
time. Most of our everyday activities, even such things as tying
one's shoes or combing one's hair, avoiding collisions with auto-
mobiles, etc., betray some modest preferences.[1] It could be argued
that an agent necessarily reveals preferences and concerns in any
of his actions and thus that it is logically impossible that an agent
who acts and makes decisions in the world (this includes almost

everyone except for people who are unconscious or in articial life
support systems) could be completely indifferent to everything.
However, this is not the case. It is at least conceivable that all of
a person's choices could be arbitrary and not based on any preferences — just as the choice to put one shoe on before the other
is arbitrary for most people.[2] (We may doubt there are any such
people, for they could not expect to live very long. If one's
decisions about such things as when to cross the street were truly
arbitrary, one would soon be run over by a motor vehicle.) People
approach the extreme of total indifference to varying degrees.
Some care about only a very few things and others care very
little about anything. The main character of Camus' *The Stranger*
comes closer to total indifference than any other fictional or
real-life character with whom I am familiar. (He represents himself as being someone for whom 'nothing matters'.) A more
moderate case is Nietzsche's "last man" from *Zarathustra* who
doesn't care very much about anything. The fact that no-one
(not even the relativist) is indifferent to everything does not
count against the claim that it is inconsistent or hypocritical for
the relativist not to be indifferent to everything. There are, as
we shall see presently, other grounds on which to reject the claim
that the hard relativist is committed to being indifferent about
everything.

It might be suggested that a person's having desires or aversions
with respect to something logically entails that he attaches positive
or negative value to it and, therefore, that simply having desires
commits one to accepting the truth of certain normative judgments. For example, deciding to become a millionaire entails that
one values money. Thus, the argument continues, the person who
decides to make money is committed to saying that it is true that
money is valuable. However, this argument confuses one's *valuing*
money with one's believing it to be valuable. To value something
is simply to have a certain kind of attitude about it. To believe

that something is valuable is to believe that it has certain properties in virtue of which it is appropriate to value it.[3]

The proponent of HMER holds that no norms, preferences, or
desires are correct in any sense that is opposed to mistaken. This
means that, for any preference that someone has, it would be
equally correct for him to have some conflicting preference
instead. Isn't the relativist thus committed to thinking that every
decision is completely arbitrary and pointless? On his own view,
isn't it completely arbitrary whether he decides to become a
Storm Trooper or a Quaker? − since the attitudes of one are
no more correct than those of the other. The choice between
different kinds of lives is just as pointless as the choice between
putting on one's right shoe before one's left or one's left shoe
before one's right − in neither case can we say that it is correct
to choose one thing rather than another. The relativist must allow
that this decision is, in an important sense, pointless but he is not
committed to being indifferent to it in the same way that most
people are indifferent to the choice of which shoe to put on first.
The relativist can care very much about this and other things,
provided that he doesn't claim that his own attitudes are correct. He can, for example, care very much about the outcome of
a baseball game, provided that he does not believe that it is correct
to prefer any particular outcome as opposed to another.

HMER commits one to the view that none of one's attitudes
about things can be objectively correct or correct in any sense
that is opposed to incorrect. It is perfectly consistent for the hard
relativist to have strong attitudes and feelings about things, provided that he does not regard them as correct in any sense that is
opposed to mistaken. There is no attitude about anything whose
correctness is entailed by HMER. *Quite to the contrary*, assuming
the connection between attitudes and norms defended in Chapter
One, HMER implies that there is nothing that is such that it is
either correct or incorrect for one to have a favorable, unfavorable

or indifferent attitude about it. Being a relativist does not commit one to the view that any attitude about the world or things in the world other than complete indifference is mistaken. Moreover, this latter view is probably mistaken. For, as we saw earlier in Section 1.1.2, there are reasons for thinking that it is false that there is anything concerning which indifference is the only correct attitude.

4.1.3. Attitudes Such as Guilt, Resentment, and "Moral Seriousness" Presuppose the Falsity of HMER

Although HMER does not commit one to rejecting or adopting any kind of global attitude about the world, there are certain characteristic moral attitudes such as guilt and resentment that have a strong cognitive component and thus presuppose the falsity of HMER.

(a) *Guilt*. Guilt involves having negative attitudes or feelings about oneself on account of one's conduct or character. This is a necessary condition of guilt but it is not sufficient. We need to add further conditions in order to distinguish guilt from such things as being displeased with oneself for having slept through the Saturday morning cartoons or being ashamed of a speech impediment. Guilt cannot be distinguished from shame or displeasure with oneself on phenomenological grounds alone. My own introspection reveals no characteristic feeling or sensation of guilt that is clearly distinguishable from shame or displeasure. (I do not know of any philosophers or psychologists who hold that guilt is distinguishable from other attitudes or emotions simply on phenomenological grounds.) Nor will it do to say that guilt is distinguishable from shame or mere displeasure with oneself simply in virtue of being more intense; for the bite of conscience is often very mild and shame and displeasure with oneself can be very intense. There is at least one (arguably two) essential difference(s) between guilt and shame. (1) Both guilt and shame are negative feelings about oneself that involve a cognitive component — the belief that one fails to "measure up" to some standard of value. Guilt, however, involves the view that one falls short of some *moral* standard. I can feel guilty about my failure to help someone in distress (since my moral standards require me to help him). However, I cannot feel guilty about my appearance or my family's poverty — unless I regard them as somehow the result of moral failings. So, guilt is distinguishable from mere shame in that it involves the belief that one character or conduct[4] is morally objectionable. (2) Guilt often involves the belief that one is *blameworthy*, i.e., worthy of disapprobation and punishment and/or ill-fortune; this accounts for the element of self-chastisement that is often present in guilt. A person who believes that he is blameworthy (there are many who never do in this permissive and relativistic age of ours) thinks himself worthy of punishment and/or ill-fortune and may even desire them in order to atone for his wrongs. He may also want to do things to "redeem himself" and make himself worthy of happiness again. The belief that one is blameworthy is often a part of guilt. Whether it is an essential feature of guilt is a question that I will leave open. Perhaps this is ultimately just a question about the meaning of words. I take it to be some evidence for the view that the belief that one is blameworthy is necessary for guilt that (at least according to some) the concept of guilt seems to have its origin in the idea that bad people will be punished in the afterlife. In the West guilt is a product of Christianity, the Greeks had no notion of guilt in our sense.[5]

Given this account of the nature of guilt, it is irrational for a person who accepts SMER to feel guilty about anything. For feeling guilty involves the belief that certain attitudes about oneself and one's personal welfare are fitting or appropriate.

(If someone deserves to be punished, then it must be correct to desire that he be punished.) A soft relativist can say that it is correct for *some people* (including himself) to disapprove of his conduct and desire that he be punished. This is something very much like guilt in the ordinary sense; what is lacking is the belief that one is worthy of everyone's disapproval or that everyone is justified in wishing one ill.

(b) *Resentment.* A consistent relativist cannot *resent* things that others do to him. Resenting what someone does is very different from simply disliking it or being angry about it. If I resent something that you have done to me I not only dislike it, I must believe that you have wronged me. Thus, resentment requires that one accept certain moral judgments. The hard relativist cannot resent anything that other people do to him, because, as we saw in Chapter Three, he cannot consistently make any moral judgments.

The position of the soft relativist is somewhat more difficult to determine. He can never say that it is objectively true that someone else has wronged him. However, he can still say that it is true for him that he was wronged. If SMER is true then we should expect to encounter cases of the following sort. x harms y and it is true for y that x wronged him, but true for x that he did not do anything wrong. Suppose also that y knows all of the above. Can he resent x? It seems more than a bit peculiar for one to resent an act that the agent has no reason to feel bad about and that he had no reason to avoid. However, as we saw at the end of Chapter Three, y can still hold that it is true for him that x wronged him and that it is appropriate for him to be angry with x. In any case, the relativist can resent the conduct of others in cases in which it is true both for him and the other person that the other person wronged him. (We should also expect there to be cases of this sort.)

(c) *Taking moral questions seriously.* A hard relativist can have no reason to be critical about the sorts of moral and normative standards that he accepts; nor can he have reason to take moral questions seriously. Many people devote considerable energy and attention to the choice or reconsideration of their normative views. Consider, for example, the deliberation and soul-searching that some people engage in while trying to get clear about the morality of such things as abortion and war. They may attempt to obtain additional factual information, discuss and debate these questions with other people and, in rare cases, even turn to philosophy. They are not content to adopt or revise norms in an arbitrary way. On our ordinary objectivist assumptions this makes perfect sense. We subject our views to careful scrutiny because they are liable to be in error. Does it make any sense for a hard relativist to be critical of his own norms or attitudes? Suppose that a hard relativist feels hatred for _____. According to the relativist there is no possibility that his attitude about _____ is mistaken. The only reason that he can have for subjecting this attitude to critical scrutiny is the desire that his attitudes about such things be consistent with his more basic attitudes and desires. Perhaps his most basic concern is love for his kinsman. In that case, he will attempt to determine whether or not he is related to _____. So, the hard relativist can raise questions about some of his desires and values in order to make them more consistent with his basic desires or his total system of desires, but he cannot have any reason to trouble himself about this most basic desires and attitudes. To say that the relativist can have *no reason* to scrutinize his entire system of values and desires is not to say that it is *inconsistent* for him to do this. It is quite consistent for a hard relativist to subject his entire system of values to investigation. He can even do this in a serious and determined manner. However, his investigations cannot have the seriousness of purpose (avoiding error and aiming at the truth) that typically underlies moral investigation. The relativist may, perhaps, alter his attitudes or desires in light of such investigations. However, he will not feel that he is in any way *bound* by the outcome of those investigations. Finally, it should also be noted that the relativist's inquiry cannot be guided by any standard of truth or correctness. It is not clear what *could* guide or motivate an examination of one's beliefs if not concern for the truth.

The proponent of soft relativism can be morally earnest in the full sense, for on his view it is possible for his values and attitudes to be in error.

4.2. CAUSAL OR PSYCHOLOGICAL CONNECTIONS BETWEEN META-ETHICAL VIEWS AND ATTITUDES AND FIRST-ORDER NORMATIVE STANDARDS

Granted that HMER does not commit one to giving up one's basic desires and attitudes about the world, the acceptance of this view often has a profound effect on people's lives. It often causes individuals to alter the content of their values and to view the things that they value as being somehow less significant. It is important to ask how the character of our evaluations and attitudes is determined by our views as to their status. The sort of person whose first order attitudes are most dependent on his views as to their status is someone whose valuations of things are at variance with his instinctive attitudes concerning them.

4.2.1. The Status of Aesthetic Standards

Consider the following example. *A* and *B* are both devoted to the opera. *A* derives great pleasure from going to the opera, in fact she enjoys it more than any other activity. She would persist in her devotion to the opera, even if she ceased to believe that it is correct for her to prefer the opera to such things as AM radio and commercial television. I am assuming that her enjoyment of the opera is not significantly affected by her views as to its value. For example, her enjoyment is not enhanced by feeling superior to those who prefer "lesser" forms of entertainment. *B*, on the other hand, does not particularly enjoy opera – he gets far more pleasure from watching commercial television. He prefers opera to TV because he thinks that opera is better. (For my purposes here it is important to stipulate that he is not motivated by the desire to appear cultured or gain status in the eyes of others – that is a very different kind of motivation than the desire to do what is most worthwhile or valuable.) *B* believes that only people with poor taste prefer television to opera. It is likely that his devotion to opera would be seriously undermined if he were to embrace HMER and as a result cease to believe that it is in any sense true that opera is better than TV or that it is correct to prefer it to TV.

4.2.2. The Likely Consequences of One's Adopting HMER

The same sorts of things can be said about one's moral commitments. If a person's instinctive desires and preferences are consistent with his basic moral principles, then it is likely that his moral commitments will be relatively independent of his views as to the status of moral principles. On the other hand, if he is the sort of person whose principles are greatly at variance with his instinctive desires and sentiments, then it is likely that his moral commitments are dependent on his meta-ethical views. Let us consider an example of the sort of person whose sentiments are very much in harmony with his principles. *A* accepts and acts in accordance with the principle of utility. His actions are not motivated so much by a desire to do what is right as by simple benevolence and sympathy for others. He is pleased by the welfare of other creatures and distressed by their suffering and ill-fortune.

(*A* resembles the Aristotelian ideal of the virtuous person in several important respects.[6]) It is likely that *A* would continue to be committed to helping his fellow creatures, even if he were to come to accept HMER. (In this case we might say that his commitment to helping others is no longer a *moral* commitment.) Consider also an example of the sort of person whose moral principles are greatly at variance with his instinctive desires. *B* is a conscientious utilitarian who frequently sacrifices his own interests for the sake of others. He has little sympathy for the suffering of other creatures and he does not derive any particular satisfaction from helping them. He is often tempted to act in his own self-interest rather than follow the principle of utility. He is not motivated by a concern for others, but rather the desire to do as he ought. (*B* bears some resemblance to the Kantian ideal. According to Kant, the person who does his duty from a sense of duty in spite of inclinations to the contrary is more praiseworthy than someone who does his duty simply as a matter of inclination.[7]) It is likely that *B*'s commitment to helping others would greatly diminish if he were to accept HMER and thus also cease to believe that it is true that he ought to act in accordance with the principle of utility. He would no longer have any motivation to promote the general welfare when doing so is contrary to his own self-interest. To illustrate this more graphically, let us suppose that *B* has an intense hatred of Jews and relishes the thought of their extermination. However, he believes in the objective correctness of a set of principles that forbids the harming of Jews or the members of any other groups. Because of this, he believes that his desires concerning the Jews are incorrect and inappropriate. Should he come to accept HMER he would no longer believe that those principles are correct and would no longer have any non-prudential reasons or motives for restraining his hostile impulses toward Jews.

The foregoing shows that there is some measure of both truth and falsehood in the familiar claim that the abandonment of belief in the objectivity of morals will result in a general deterioration of standards of conduct.[8] If one desires to do things that one believes to be prohibited then it is likely that one will do them if one comes to believe that nothing is prohibited (or that it is not true that anything is prohibited). On the other hand, if one has no particular desire to do what one believes to be prohibited, then it is unlikely that one will do those things if one ceases to believe that they are prohibited (or ceases to believe that it is true that they are prohibited). A person who fits the Kantian ideal is very likely to be corrupted by relativistic meta-ethical views; those who fit the Aristotelian ideal are relatively immune to such corruption.

Our natural sympathies are severely limited. Most of us are benevolently disposed towards members of our own families and to friends and acquaintances. Some have a more wide-ranging benevolence. But few humans are strongly inclined to be concerned with the welfare of society or humanity as a whole. Most of us are more greatly moved by the news of a friend's loss of employment than the news of the deaths of tens of thousands of people in distant lands. This means that our natural sympathies are not sufficient to prevent us from acting in ways which tend to worsen the human condition. According to Warnock, the primary purpose or "object" of morality is to give us motives for acting in ways that tend to improve the human condition in addition to those motives provided by our natural sympathies.[9] The foregoing shows that morality cannot have the kind of motivational power that Warnock takes to be its *raison d'être* for a consistent hard relativist. Moral judgments cannot supply additional motivation over and above our natural inclinations unless one takes them to be correct in some sense that is opposed to mistaken. (Of course, as we saw in Chapter Three the hard relativist cannot consistently accept any moral judgments.) Because of limitations in our 'natural virtues', benevolence, and generosity, etc., the human race is better off on account of the fact that most of us believe that moral judgments are correct in a sense that is opposed to mistaken.[10]

4.2.3. The Effects of Accepting SMER

What are the likely effects of adopting SMER? What, for example, has it done to me? To what extent are one's attitudes and desires dependent on one's believing that they are objectively correct? It would be helpful to consider the two cases that were discussed in connection with HMER.

Our first example concerns two people who are devoted to the opera. A's devotion to the opera is a matter of basic inclination and taste. It is not dependent on her believing that it is objectively correct (or correct in any other sense) to prefer opera to other forms of entertainment. Her devotion to the opera would not be diminished if she were to accept SMER. (As we have seen, her devotion would not be affected by the more radical move to HMER). If B were to become a soft relativist it is quite possible that he would continue his interest in the opera on the grounds that it is correct for him (even if not everyone else) to think that the opera is better than other forms of entertainment. However, there are several ways in which his devotion might be undermined by becoming a relativist. If he becomes a soft relativist and ceases to believe that the correctness of his own views about opera consists simply in any objective features of opera itself, he *may* (but need not) adopt alternative standards of correctness that do not imply that it is correct for him to prefer opera. He may, for example, come to believe that it is correct for one to prefer whatever forms of entertainment give one the most enjoyment. There may also be some kind of herd instinct that is a factor in his devotion to the opera and which would be eliminated if he adopted SMER. Some people may be more moved or inspired by judments that they believe to be correct for everyone than judgments which they think are merely true for themselves.

Let us now consider the example of our two utilitarians — *A* who acts in accordance with the principle of utility out of benevolence and *B* who follows it for the sake of doing his duty. As I argued earlier, *A*'s conduct is unlikely to be greatly affected if he becomes a hard relativist. The less radical move to soft relativism would presumably not have a significant effect either — if anything it should have less of an effect. What about *B*? Can his desire to do his duty and act so as to be worthy of approval continue to provide him with motivation to act in accordance with the principle of utility if he becomes a weak relativist? If he comes to think that it is only true for him and some other people that he ought to act so as to promote the general welfare, he will still be motivated to follow the principle of utility in order to act in a way that is worthy of his own approval. However, the desire to act in a way that is worthy of everyone's approval can no longer motivate him. For, according to SMER, there is nothing that he or anyone else can do that is worthy of everyone's approval. However, speaking for myself, the ability of moral considerations to overcome my limited sympathies is quite undiminished. The idea that I would be moved to do something if I were to represent adequately all of the relevant facts motivates me as much, if not more, than the belief that certain acts are required by objective moral laws used to motivate me.

NIETZSCHE ON THE GENEALOGY OF MORALS

The version of the ideal observer theory defended in Chapter Two depends importantly on the Nietzschean view that certain kinds of moral views have their origins in hatred, envy, and self-deception and that this fact somehow discredits those views. Here, I think that it would be appropriate to say something more about Nietzsche's views concerning the genealogy of morals.

Nietzsche's writings abound with speculations about the origins of moral ideals. Moral ideals are claimed to be a product of various psychological and "physiological" factors — some are claimed to be the product of strength, others the product of weakness. Among other things, Nietzsche claims that Christian morality and certain other ideals to which he is opposed have their origin in suppressed hatred and envy. In spite of the prominence of 'genetic' considerations in Nietzsche's moral philosophy, commentators have had very little to say about the purpose and significance of his claims about the genealogy of morals. It remains unclear what these claims are intended to establish. What, for example, is the point of arguing that Christian morality is the product of *ressentiment*? Is it supposed to show that Christian morality is false? Commentators make note of Nietzsche's views about the genealogy of morals and many pay particular attention to his notion of *ressentiment*. However, none of the major English-language commentators on Nietzsche's moral philosophy, Brinton, Copleston, Danto, Hollingdale, Kaufmann, Morgan, or Wilcox, attempt to answer any of the above questions. In *Ressentiment*, Scheler argues that moral judgments that constitute an expression of *ressentiment* are, in some sense, mistaken or incorrect. This is

so, he claims, because *ressentiment* distorts or perverts our awareness of an eternal and objective realm of values (p. 73). Whatever
the merits of this view, it is not a plausible interpretation of
Nietzsche — nor is it intended to be. (Nietzsche would surely
reject the kind of moral realism presupposed by Scheler's view.)
Here, I will present what I take to be the most significant claims
that Nietzsche makes concerning the origins of moral ideals and
then argue that, although the texts do not support a definitive
interpretation, there is *some* reason to suppose that he takes facts
about the origins of certain moral views to constitute grounds
for thinking that they are incorrect.

I.1. NIETZSCHE'S CLAIMS CONCERNING
THE GENEALOGY OF MORALS

(1) Nietzsche claims that certain kinds of normative views are
the products of repressed or displaced hostility. Such views
constitute an outlet and source of gratification for feelings of
hatred and revenge. Conventional morality, particularly Christian
morality, places a negative valuation on the characteristics of
the strong and noble: pride, the will to rule, and aggressiveness.
To adopt conventional morality is to provide oneself with a
pretext for making negative judgments about "higher" types of
individuals. Thus conventional morality is, or can be, an expression of hatred by the weak for the strong.

Moral judgments and condemnations constitute the favorite revenge of the
spiritually limited against those less limited . . . (*BG&E*, 147).

Morality consequently taught men to hate and despise most profoundly
what is the basic character trait of those who rule: their will to power (*WP*,
36—37).

Morality as a means of seduction . . . a pretext is sought to introduce an
insatiable thirst for revenge as a moral-religious duty. Hatred for the ruling
order seeks to sanctify itself (*WP*, 190).

The slave revolt in morality begins when *ressentiment* itself becomes creative and gives birth to values: the *ressentiment* of natures that are denied the true reaction, that of deeds, and compensate themselves with an imaginary revenge (*GM*, 36; also see *TI*, 58; *GM*, 34, 40, 74, and 124; *BG&E*, 99; *DD*, 36; *Z*, 147 and 211–212; *AC*, 153–160 and 179; and *WP*, 108, 160, 202, 216, and 253).[1]

I take it that Nietzsche is claiming that suppressed hatred is a motivating factor both in the origin and acceptance of conventional values. (He does not always distinguish between the kinds of psychological factors that motivated the creator of a particular ideal and the motivations that others may have for accepting it.)

Nietzsche denies the validity or applicability of the notions of guilt and moral praiseworthiness and blameworthiness.[2] He also denies the existence of free will. According to Nietzsche, the acceptance of these notions has its origins in the desire to hurt others. We believe in guilt and free will etc., because we want an excuse or justification for hurting others.

The error of free will . . . wherever responsibilities are sought it is usually the instinct of wanting to judge and punish which is at work. . . . the doctrine of the will has been invented essentially for the purpose of punishment, that is, because one wanted to impute guilt. . . . Men were considered "free" so that they might be judged and punished — so that they might become *guilty* . . . Christianity is the metaphysics of the hangman (*TI*, 499–500 in *The Portable Nietzsche*; also see *GM*, 45 and *WP*, 402).

(2) Nietzsche claims that negative evaluations of many things result from an inability to obtain the things in question. When someone demeans the value of things that he can't have or can't do we suspect that his judgment is just 'sour grapes' and thus, in some sense, dishonest or insincere. Saint Paul couldn't live in accordance with the Jewish law so he rejected it and became a Christian (*DD*, 60). Likewise Luther's doctrine of "Justification by Faith" springs from his own inability to perform Christian works (*WP*, 114; also see *GS*, 312). At bottom the weak instinc-

tively yearn for nobler ideals but they disparage them because they know that they are incapable of attaining them.

(3) Conventional morality is also characterized by the very similar phenomenon of 'making a virtue of necessity' or 'making something sweet out of a lemon'. The weak person is incapable of revenge, pride, harming others, or being independent. He makes a virtue of these limitations and calls them "forgiveness", "humility", "forebearance", "obedience", and "loyalty".

When the oppressed, downtrodden, outraged exhort one another with the vengeful cunning of impotence: "let us be different from the evil, namely good! ..." ... this ... really amounts to no more than: "We weak ones are, after all weak; it would be good if we did nothing *for which we are not strong enough*"; but this dry matter of fact, this prudence of the lowest order which even insects possess (posing as dead, when in great danger, so as not to do "too much"), has, thanks to the counterfeit and self-deception of impotence, clad itself in the ostentatious garb of the virtue of quiet calm resignation, just as if the weakness of the weak — that is to say their *essence*, their affects, their sole ineluctable, irremovable reality — were a voluntary achievement, willed, chosen, a *deed*, a *meritorious* act (*GM*, 46).

Verily, I have often laughed at the weaklings who thought themselves good because they had no claws (*Z*, 230).

Weakness is being lied into something *meritorious* . . . and impotence which does not requite into 'goodness of heart'; anxious lowliness into 'humility'; subjection to those one hates into 'obedience' . . . The inoffensiveness of the weak man, even the cowardice of which he has so much, his lingering at the door, his being ineluctably compelled to wait, here acquire flattering names, such as 'patience,' and are even called virtue itself; his inability for revenge is called unwillingness to revenge, perhaps even forgiveness ('for they know not what they do — we alone know what *they* do!') They also speak of 'loving one's enemies' and sweat as they do" (*GM*, 47; also see *WP*, 167, 183, 196, and 398).

(4) People tend to make moral judgments that satisfy their emotional needs. Most importantly, we are inclined to make

judgments that allow us to have a favorable opinion of ourselves. (See *WP*, 216; *HA* Vol. I, 78 and *BG&E*, 99). Evaluations of oneself typically involve either implicit or explicit comparisons with other people; our self-esteem tends to be a function of how we believe that we compare with others. Thus, we may have a need or predilection to make unfavorable evaluations of other people. Scheler discusses this at some length (*Ressentiment*, 46–55).

(5) The greater portion of Nietzsche's work on the origin of moral ideals concerns the allegedly unsavory origins of moral codes that he rejects. He also makes some brief observations about the origins of what he calls "master moralities". (Nietzsche would give at least qualified approval of such views.) Before noting these observations I will try to explain Nietzsche's distinction between "master morality" and "slave morality". According to Nietzsche, there are two basic types of moralities: master morality (the morality of the rulers) and slave morality (the morality of the ruled) (*BG&E*, 204). These are idealized notions – most, if not all, moral codes display aspects of each (*BG&E*, 204). Kaufmann suggests that the heroic morality of Homer's *Iliad* and the morality of the New Testament are reasonably good examples of the pure master and slave types (see his note to the text *BG&E*, 206). One of the most fundamental differences between master morality and slave morality is that they employ different basic normative notions. The basic concepts in master morality are good and bad (or noble and contemptible); for slave morality the basic notions are good and evil (*BG&E*, 204 and *GM*, 36–7). The difference in basic concepts is connected with differences in origins. In slave morality the concept of bad or evil is primary. Slave morality is essentially reactive – it is an expression of the slaves' hatred for their masters (*GM*, 36–7). Master morality, on the other hand, has its origins in "self-glorification" and "triumphant self-affirmation". The noble type of individual declares his own

characteristics to be good; for him the concept of bad is merely an afterthought (*GM*, 36–7 and *BG&E*, 205).

I.2. WHAT ARE NIETZSCHE'S GENETIC CLAIMS INTENDED TO SHOW?

Nietzsche's observations about the origins of Christian Morality and the conventional morality of his time are quite familiar, if not notorious. However, their purpose and their place in his philosophy is unclear. This issue is rarely, if ever, addressed by Nietzsche scholars. I shall now venture an interpretation of the purpose(s) of Nietzsche's inquiry into the genealogy of morals. Among other things, I shall argue that there is a *prima facie* case for thinking that he takes facts about the genesis of certain normative views to constitute grounds for supposing them to be incorrect. I shall restrict myself to discussing his views as to the significance of what he alleges to be the unsavory origins of moral ideals to which he is opposed.

(1) There are a number of places in which Nietzsche says that moral judgments are symptoms of underlying "physiological" conditions — health or sickness, weakness or strength, and poverty or abundance (*WP*, 148, 149, and 326; *GM*, 17; and *GS*, 329). In some places he claims that moral judgments are "merely" symptoms of "physiological" states (*BG&E*, 100; and *TI*, 30, 45, and 55). This suggests that the (or a) purpose of his genetic investigations is to determine the connection between moral views and physiological conditions. For Nietzsche, this is no mere academic exercise. For health and sickness and strength and weakness are the most basic normative notions in his scheme of things. The good is whatever is strong and healthy or whatever promotes strength and health; the bad is whatever is weak or sick or promotes weakness and sickness.[3] Thus, given all of this, Nietzsche's genetic claims can justify him in making unfavorable first-order

normative judgments about those who accept ideals to which he is opposed. However, none of these considerations suggests any way in which facts about the origin of values can justify ultimate normative standards.

(2) There is a passage in *The Will to Power* in which Nietzsche seems to suggest that the value of his genetic investigations consists solely in their persuasive power. The discovery of the shameful origin of conventional morality arouses in us a feeling of diminished value and thus prepares the way for a more critical attitude about it (p. 148). This more critical attitude involves seeing morality as merely a means to enhance life. Life should not be subordinated to the claims of morality, rather morality should be subordinate to "life".

(3) The most important question concerning the aims of Nietzsche's genetic investigations is whether he takes the allegedly unsavory origins of conventional norms to constitute any kind of reason for denying the truth or correctness of those norms. The texts do not yield a definite answer. Nowhere does Nietzsche explicitly claim that facts about the origin of moral judgments can establish their incorrectness. However, there are several passages in which he *seems* to imply that his genetic investigations provide reasons for thinking that certain views are incorrect:

When the socialist with a fine indignation demands "justice," "right," "equal rights," he is merely acting under the impress of his inadequate culture that cannot explain why he is suffering: on the other hand, he enjoys himself; if he felt better he would refrain from crying out: he would then find pleasure in other things. The same applies to the Christian: he condemns, disparages, curses the "world" — himself not excluded. But that is no reason for taking his clamor seriously. In both cases we are in the presence of invalids who feel better crying out, for whom defamation is a relief (*WP*, 202; also see *GS*, 24).

or

Why do you consider this, precisely this, right?

"Because this is what my conscience tells me; and the voice of conscience is never immoral, for it alone determines what is to be moral."

But why do you *listen* to the voice of your conscience? And what gives you the right to consider such a judgment true and infallible? . . .

or

For all that, the *firmness of your moral judgment could be* evidence of your personal abjectness, of impersonality; your "moral strength" might have its source in your stubborness − or in your inability to envisage new ideals. And, briefly, if you had thought more subltly, observed better, and learned more, you certainly would not go on calling this "duty" of yours and this conscience of yours duty and conscience. Your understanding *of the manner in which moral judgments have originated* would spoil these grand words for you, just as other grand words like "sin" and "salvation of the soul" and "redemption" have been spoiled for you (*GS*, 263−264).

War on all presuppositions on the basis of which one has invented a true world. Among these is the presupposition that moral values are the supreme values.

The supremacy of moral valuation would be refuted if it could be shown to be the consequence of an immoral valuation − as a special case of immorality − it would thus reduce itself to an appearance, and as an appearance it would cease to have any right as such to condemn appearance (*WP*, 314; also see *WP*, 189).

In the second passage Nietzsche seems to suggest that the truth or correctness of our moral judgments is called into question by facts about their origin. In the latter passage I take Nietzsche to be saying that the fact that moral values arise only as a result of inclinations and training that are immoral according to those very values themselves (Nietzsche claims this in a number of places − *WP*, 156, 172, 214, 219 and *TI*, 59), means that we have no reason to suppose that moral values have any basis in the nature of things or that they are higher than other sorts of values. Nietzsche usually uses the term 'moral' in a very narrow sense; his discussion of master morality is an exception to this. He does not count his own values and normative standards as moral values or moral standards.[4] 'Morality' for Nietzsche refers to standards of good and evil. Morality countenances judgments of praiseworthiness or merit and blameworthiness or guilt and thus presupposes the existence of free will. Nietzsche suggests that we abandon moral standards or standards of good and evil, but retain or develop standards of good and bad (*GM*, 54 and *GS*, 265–6). For other places in which he distinguishes between moral and non-moral values, see *WP*, 149, 164, 201, 255, 314, 521; and *EH*, 290.

(4) Nietzsche's claims to the effect that certain moral values can only be inculcated in society by means that are immoral on their own terms suggest the following argument; 'People cannot be trained or motivated to follow a certain moral code (c) unless those training or motivating them violate (c), themselves. From this it follows that it cannot be correct to say that everyone ought to follow (c). For, by hypothesis, that is not a possible state of affairs and 'ought' implies 'can'.' I take this to be a valid argument and that it is valid is an additional reason for believing that Nietzsche thinks that facts about the origins of certain views establish the incorrectness of those views. It might be objected that the argument depends upon an equivocation. The statement that everyone ought to follow (c) is ambiguous between the following:

(1)   Each person ought to follow (c).

and

(2)   It ought to be the case that everyone follows (c).

Nietzsche's claim that conventional morality can only be taught through means that are immoral according to its own standards entails the following:

(3)   If anyone follows (c) then someone violates (c).

The principle that 'ought implies can' entails the following:

(4)   If x ought to do y then x can do y, and if it ought to be the case that x, then it can be the case that x.

The conjunction of (3) and (4) entails that (2) is false. But the proponent of conventional morality does not need to hold (2); he only needs to hold (1) and the falsity of (1) is not entailed by (3) and (4). However, the proponent of conventional morality is also committed to holding such things as the following:

(5)   Each person ought to follow (c), even if everyone else follows and has followed (c).

This statement is inconsistent with the conjunction of (3) and (4). Therefore it seems as if Nietzsche's claims about the immorality of conventional moral training suggest a valid argument for the falsity of certain claims of conventional morality. Although I take the foregoing to be a valid argument, there are few, if any, actual cases in which one could employ this argument. For it would be extremely difficult to show that people can be trained or motivated to adhere to a certain moral code only by means that are contrary to the code itself. It would not be enough to show that those who *in fact* act in accordance with the code were trained by means which were incompatible with the code.

Note the distinction between (1) 'This set of moral principles is incorrect, because those who accept it are motivated by hatred and envy' and (2) 'This set of principles is incorrect, because it could *only* be accepted by someone who was motivated by hatred and envy'. (The arguments of Chapter Two provide support for (2), or something like (2), but not for (1).) Nietzsche fails to distinguish between (1) and (2) and one cannot safely attribute either to him. All that can be said is that there is *some* reason to think that he believes that the fact that people's acceptance of certain views is in some sense dependent on their being motivated by hatred and envy shows that those views are incorrect.

NORMATIVE RELATIVISM AND NIHILISM

In Chapter Three, I argued that several common versions of meta-ethical relativism are nihilistic views in the sense that it is inconsistent for someone who holds such a view to make any moral judgments. Here I shall argue that several common versions of normative relativism are nihilistic views in a somewhat different sense — it is inconsistent for the normative relativist to make any moral judgments about himself or his own conduct. Normative relativism is the view that the moral status of a person and what he does is relative to his own moral standards or the moral standards of the society of which he is a member. There are many possible versions of normative relativism among which are the following:

(1) It is right for S to do x iff he believes that it is right for him to do it, wrong for S to do x iff he believes that it is wrong for him to do it, and obligatory for S to do x iff he believes that it is obligatory for him to do x.[1]

(2) It is right (wrong, obligatory) for S to do x iff this is entailed by the conjunction of his basic moral principles and the set of true factual statements that describes S's situation and the alternative courses of action open to him at the time.[2]

(3) S's doing x is right (wrong, obligatory) iff this is entailed by the conjunction of the basic moral principles of the society of which he is a member and the set of true factual statements that describes S's situation and

157

the alternative courses of action open to him at the time.[3]

(4) S's doing x is right (wrong, obligatory) iff this is entailed by the conjunction of the basic moral principles of the society in which he performs x and the set of true factual statements that describes the alternative courses of action open to S at the time. (Those who subscribe to some version of the principle 'when in Rome do as a Roman' would prefer (4) to (3).)[4]

(5) S is a good (bad, indifferent) person iff he believes that he is good (bad, indifferent). A particular characteristic of (x) of S is good (bad, indifferent) iff S believes that x is good (bad, indifferent).

(6) S is a good (bad, indifferent) person iff the conjunction of his basic moral principles and the set of true factual statements that describes him entails that he is a good (bad, indifferent) person. A particular characteristic (x) of S is good (bad, indifferent) iff the conjunction of his basic moral principles and the set of true factual statements that describes S entails that x is good (bad, indifferent).

(7) S is a good (bad, indifferent) person iff the conjunction of the basic moral principles of the society of which he is a member and the set of true factual statements that describes S entails that S is good (bad, indifferent). A particular characteristic (x) of S is good (bad, indifferent) iff the conjunction of the basic moral principles of the society of which S is a member and the set of true factual statements that describes S entails that x is good (bad, indifferent).

According to (1) nothing that a person does can be right or wrong or obligatory unless he believes that it would be right or wrong or obligatory for him to do certain things. But if a person accepts (1), then it is inconsistent for him to have any beliefs of this sort. Therefore, (1) implies that if a person accepts (1) and is consistent, then nothing that he does can be right or wrong or obligatory. The foregoing argument depends upon the assumption that if a person accepts (1), then it is inconsistent for him to have any beliefs to the effect that it would be right or wrong or obligatory for him to do certain things. In order to believe that one's doing something is right or wrong or obligatory one must believe that it would be a mistake for one to believe anything that is opposed to this. For example, I cannot be said to believe that I ought to be kind to my cat unless I believe that it would be a mistake for me to think that I have no obligation to be kind to her — otherwise I could not be said to believe one thing rather than the other. It is not just that if one believes x one must think that it would be a mistake for one to accept *both* x and not-x, but that in order to believe x one must think that it would be a mistake for one to believe not-x *instead of* x. (See Section 3.3.) (1) implies that it can never be a mistake for a person to accept one judgment about what he ought to do as opposed to another. For, according to (1), any beliefs that one has to the effect that it is right or wrong or obligatory for one to do something are guaranteed to be correct. If one believes that it would be right (or wrong) for one to do something, then it must be the case that it would be right (or wrong) for one to do it. Thus, if a person accepts (1) he can never say that it would be incorrect for him to accept one particular judgment about what he ought to do as opposed to another. Therefore, in order to be consistent such an individual cannot have any beliefs to the effect that it is right or wrong for him to do certain things. Precisely the same kind of argument can be given to show that a person who accepts (5) cannot make any judgments to the effect that he or any character-istic that he possesses is good, bad or indifferent.

(2) also commits one to the view that nothing that one does can be right or wrong or obligatory. (2) implies that nothing one does can be right or wrong or obligatory unless one accepts principles of right and wrong other than (2). However, one who accepts (2) cannot consistently accept any of the requisite sorts of principles. There are moral principles that have implications concerning what is right or wrong or obligatory for one to do, e.g., 'everyone should always do whatever will have the best consequences' and 'I should always do whatever will have the best consequences'. (2) implies that if I accept such a principle then I should always act so as to bring about the best possible consequences. However, such principles are, themselves, inconsisitent with (2). For they imply that I should always do whatever will have the best conse-quences, even if my doing so is not required by my basic moral principles. The only kinds of moral principles that have implica-tions concerning what it would be right or wrong for me to do that are consistent with (2) are of the following sort: 'A person should always do whatever will have the best consequences, *provided that his doing so is required by his basic moral princi-ples*'. But such principles add nothing to (2). If this or if this and (2) are the only sorts of moral principles that one accepts, then (2) implies that one has no moral obligations. Similar argu-ments can be given to show that a person who accepts (6) cannot make any moral judgments to the effect that he or any character-istic that he possesses is good, bad or indifferent.

Those who accept either (1) or (2) can still make judgments to the effect that it would be right or wrong or obligatory for *others* to do certain things. Other people may have beliefs or accept principles according to which their doing certain things would be right or wrong or obligatory. But those who accept either (1) or (2) must also say that no one who consistently adheres to the correct normative view ((1) or (2)) can have such beliefs or accept such principles. Those who accept either (1) or (2) are committed to the most peculiar view that its being the case that there are things that it would be right or wrong or obligatory for someone to do is ultimately dependent on that person's having made some kind of error.

The individualistic versions of normative relativism, i.e., those versions of normative relativism according to which the goodness or badness of a person or the rightness or wrongness of his actions is relative to his own moral standards ((1), (2), (5), and (6)), are nihilistic theories in the sense that a person who accepts such a view cannot consistently make any moral judgments about his own moral status. The versions of normative relativism according to which right and wrong and good and bad are relative to the moral standards of a larger society ((3), (4), and (7)) do not have such implications. An individual who accepts (3) or (4) can say that there are acts that it would be right or wrong or obligatory for him to do — provided that most of the other people in his society or the society in which the act is performed accept principles according to which his doing certain things would be right or wrong.

Here it is appropriate to ask whether either (3) or (4) implies that the existence of right and wrong and moral obligation depends on people's having committed some kind of error. Suppose that everyone accepts (3) or (4). Suppose also, and this is important, that everyone knows that everyone else accepts (3) or (4). What kinds of principles would people adopt in these circumstances? According to (3) or (4), any moral principle that is inconsistent with the basic moral principles of the society of which one is a member or the principles of the society in which one is located is liable to yield incorrect moral judgments. So, one will accept a moral principle only if one believes that most of the members of the society accept it as well. Each person knows that the others will adopt principles only if they believe that most others will adopt them also. It might seem that in this situation no one will have reason to think that there is any particular set of principles that most others will adopt and, therefore, that no one will adopt any principles at all. But this is not the case. In this situation people could still *agree* to adopt a particular set of principles. Once the members of a society have agreed to adopt a set of principles then one can adopt it with the assurance that most others do so as well. In this case there is little danger that people will go back on their agreement, since all are presumed to have the desire to adopt the same principles as most other people. In thinking about this case it is helpful to consider the following analogous situation. Voters are to choose between candidates x and y. Suppose that each voter has the following motivation: he will not vote for anyone unless he thinks that he is voting for the same candidate as most other people. In this situation it is very likely that no one will vote for anyone. However, voters can be assured of voting with the majority if most of them agree to vote in a particular way beforehand. Similar arguments can be given to show that it is consistent for an individual who accepts (7) to make judgments about his own goodness or badness and that he is not committed to holding that its being the case that there is anyone about whom such judgments can be correctly made is ultimately dependent on people's having committed some kind of error.

HARE'S VERSION OF THE IDEAL OBSERVER THEORY

In the most recent statement of his moral theory, *Moral Thinking*, R. M. Hare defends what amounts to a version of the ideal observer theory. According to Hare, the truth or correctness of a moral judgment depends on its acceptability to rational inquirers. Hare thinks that all rational inquirers will be constrained to make the same moral judgments about all cases, if they make any moral judgments at all. (According to Hare, rational considerations alone cannot compel us to make moral judgments of any sort.)

I shall be maintaining that, if we assumed a perfect command of logic and of the facts, they would constrain so severely the moral evaluations that we can make, that in practice we would be bound all to agree to the same ones.[1]

After identifying the term "archangel" with "ideal observer", Hare writes the following:

Provided that we do not give it a 'subjectivist' or 'relativist' interpretation (12.1), there is no harm in saying that the right or best way for us to live or act either in general or on a particular occasion is what the archangel would pronounce to be so if he addressed himself to the question.[2]

An earlier draft of the present book was complete before I had a chance to read Hare's book. Rather than rewrite Chapter Two to give Hare's recent work the attention that it deserves, I have chosen to give a brief account of Hare's version of the IOT here. Hare thinks that fully rational moral appraisers will be so constrained that they will agree in their judgments about all moral issues. Hare also argues that archangels or ideal observers suitably constrained by facts and logic will be compelled to make moral judgments that are in accordance with the principle of utility.

163

Unlike Hare I do not think that utilitarianism or any other substantive moral theory about what makes things good or bad or
right or wrong can be derived from the ideal observer theory.
I will now attempt to state Hare's argument as best I can and
then briefly indicate points of disagreement. I will not undertake
an attempt to refute Hare; nor will I discuss his splendid defense
of utilitarianism against intuitionist and "common sense" objections.

Hare's argument depends on the plausibility of his analysis
of the meaning of moral judgments. According to Hare, moral
judgments are prescriptions that are "universalizable" and "overriding".[3] Moral judgments prescribe actions in just the same way
that commands and requests do. They differ from mere commands
or requests, e.g., 'close the door', in that they are universalizable
and overriding. To say that moral judgments are universalizable
means roughly that if one makes a moral judgment about a particular case, one is committed to making exactly the same moral
judgment about any similar case, unless there is a relevant difference between the two cases. To say that moral judgments are
overriding means that one takes the prescriptions expressed in the
moral judgments that one accepts as prescriptions that ought to
be followed in cases of conflict with other sorts of prescriptions,
e.g., conflicts between morality and counsels of prudence and
conflicts between morality and the law or morality and etiquette.
According to Hare, one of the rational constraints that the universalizability of moral judgments imposes on moral appraisers is that
if one makes a moral judgment about a particular case, it must be
the case that one would be willing to make the same judgment
about the case if one occupied the position or place of any of the
parties who might be affected by the action in question. So, for
example, if one says that slavery is morally permissible it must be
the case that one would be willing to say that slavery is morally
permissible if one were a slave.[4] Another important and highly

controversial feature of Hare's theory (a feature that I criticized earlier, in Sections 1.2.7–1.2.9), is his claim that a necessary condition of one's accepting a moral judgment is that one act in accordance with it whenever it is possible for one to do so.[5] Hare holds that a necessary condition of S's accepting a moral principle to the affect that he ought to do x is that he do x if it is in his power to do it and he is aware that the principle in question commits him to doing x. If this is taken together with the requirement of universalizability, we get the result that it must be the case that S would prefer or 'will' that x be performed in this situation, even if he were in the position of one of the other parties affected by his doing x. So, if I say that a master is morally obligated to keep his slaves in bondage, it must be the case that I would prefer that I be kept in bondage myself if I were a slave. If I say that slavery is morally permissible (but not obligatory) then it must be the case that I would be willing to be either freed or kept in bondage if I were a slave. The vast majority of us would strongly prefer that we not be kept as slaves ·under almost any circumstances. Therefore, most people are rationally constrained to reject the judgment that slavery is morally permissible or morally obligatory. This is the kind of argument developed at length by Hare in *Freedom and Reason*.

A major problem with this kind of argument that Hare himself notes in *Freedom and Reason* is that one might be so fanatically devoted to a perverted ideal that one would consent to policies that advance the ideal, even if one were to find oneself in the position of someone who might be grievously harmed by that ideal. Hare gives the example of the Nazi who discovers that he is Jewish and consents to his own extermination.[6] The machinery of *Freedom and Reason* does not seem to offer any satisfactory way of dealing with such cases. Hare and many others regard this as a serious shortcoming of his earlier view. One of the things that allows the case of the "fanatic" to be a problem for the position defended in *Freedom and Reason* is that when the fanatic imagines himself in the position of the person who might be his victim he retains his present fanatical preferences and desires. The actual preferences of the victims to the affect that they not be harmed are not allowed to come into play; all that is allowed to come into play are the desires that the fanatic would have if he were in their position. In *Moral Thinking*, Hare, in effect, argues that when we place ourselves in the position of another person and ask whether we can still accept the prescriptions that we make we must take on the other person's preferences and desires. This requirement is justified on the grounds that we can't really know what the other person's position is like *for him* unless we have the same desires and aversions that he has.

I am to imagine myself in his situation with *his preferences. Unless I have an equal aversion to myself suffering*, forthwith, what he is suffering or going to suffer, I cannot really be knowing, or even believing, that being in his situation would be like *that*.[7]

I cannot know the extent and quality of others' sufferings and, in general, motivations and preferences without having equal motivations with regard to what should happen to me, were I in their places, with their motivations and preferences.[8]

Here I find Hare's argument very difficult to follow. Consider a policy that benefits some and adversely affects others, e.g., slavery. Suppose that I put myself in the position of the slaveowners and acquire their desires and aversions. I will prefer that the institution of slavery be continued. If I put myself in the position of the slave and acquire his desires and aversions I will be unwilling to see the practice of slavery continue. If I take on the preferences of the different individuals affected by the institution of slavery at different times I will have different preferences about the continuation of slavery at different times. This is clearly not what Hare has in mind in requiring that we be willing to "universalize" our principles. What he has in mind is something like the following: I take on all of the preferences of all of the affected parties *at once* and do a kind of 'summing' of these preferences. The overall preference that emerges as a result of this summing is the morally significant one — the one that counts as the one that I am willing to universalize 'irrespective of my position'. To say that correct moral judgments must be consistent with the preferences that would emerge as a result of this kind of summing is tantamount to saying that, *if we make any moral judgments at all*, we are rationally committed to making the same judgments that would follow from a 'preference version' of utilitarianism. In our present example, the preference of the slaves not to be enslaved will presumably outweigh the preferences of those who wish to see the institution of slavery perpetuated.

Hare's argument can be summarized as follows:

(1) Moral judgments must be universalizable; if one makes a moral judgment about a particular case, one must make the same judgment about all cases that are the same in all morally relevant respects, including those hypothetical cases in which one occupies the positions of the different individuals who are affected by the action or policy in question. (If a hypothetical case (c') is just like another actual or hypothetical case (c) except that a particular person occupies a position in c' that he does not occupy in c, then c and c' are identical in all morally relevant respects. The fact that a particular individual occupies a certain position in one case and a different position in another case is not a morally relevant difference. It is not a relevant difference if I am in the position of the master in one case and the position of the slave in the other.)

(2) Occupying the position of another person or "putting oneself in his shoes" requires that one understand what it would be like to be in his position.

(3) In order to understand what it would be like to be in

another person's position one must have his desires and aversions. To put oneself in the position of two or more people one must take on their preferences simultaneously.

(4) If S accepts a moral judgment or moral principle that implies that he ought to do x at t, then it must be the case that S does x at t, provided that: (1) he is aware that the judgment or principle in question commits him to doing x at t and (2) he is able to do x at t.

(5) If S accepts a moral judgment or principle that implies that he ought to do x at t, he must be willing to accept the judgment that S ought to do x at t, even if he were to occupy the position of someone else.

(6) If someone makes a judgment to the effect that S ought to do x at t, then it must be the case that he would be willing to accept the judgment that S ought to do x at t, even if he were in the position of S or some other affected party. (Hare never states this premise explicitly to my knowledge, however, it is clear that this assumption is necessary for his argument.)

(7) If one accepts a moral judgment to the affect that S ought to do x at t, then one must be willing that it be the case that S does x at t *irrespective of one's own position* among the parties who are affected by S's decision of whether or not to do x at t. ((7) follows from the conjunction of (4), (5), and (6).)

(8) The preferences that one has with respect to S's doing x at t that qualify as the ones that one would be willing to have S do 'irrespective of one's position' is the overall set of preferences that would emerge if one had all of the preferences of all the affected parties simultaneously.

(9) The sum of the preferences of the affected parties is the same sum that a 'preference version' of act-utilitarianism would

have us try to find in order to determine the rightness or wrongness of an action.

Therefore

(10) If one makes any moral judgments at all, facts and logic constrain one to make moral judgments in accordance with a preference version of utilitarianism.

Although my main purpose here is to state Hare's position rather than attempt to refute it, I will conclude with a brief statement of the points at which I am inclined to reject his argument. First, I have reservations about premise (3), which states that an adequate representation of another person's experiences requires that one have his preferences oneself. Why, for example, can't I know perfectly well what it is like for a politician to be disappointed about losing an election, even if I don't share his desire for elective office? Second, I reject premise (4), for it rules out the possibility of moral weakness and also makes the existence of amoralists and immoralists (in the sense that I defined these notions in Chapter One) a logical impossibility. Finally, in spite of a commendable effort at clarity, there are very serious difficulties with the idea of an individual summing the preferences of different people into a single preference. Hare's argument assumes that it makes sense to imagine that a single individual could have the opposed preferences of different people simultaneously. But this idea seems incoherent to me. Suppose that there is a slave who prefers the abolition of slavery to anything and a slave owner who prefers the preservation of slavery to its abolition. No single individual can have both of these sets of preferences simultaneously. Hare uses the idea that a single individual could have the preferences of more than one person at a time in order to make sense out of the notion of a 'sum of preferences'. He defines the resulting sum of the preferences of *A*, *B*, and *C* as the (overall) preferences that one would have if one had all of the preferences of *A*, *B*, and *C* simultaneously. Perhaps there is some other way of making coherent the idea of a sum of the preferences of different people, but Hare fails to provide us with such a way.

NOTES

CHAPTER ONE

1 Franz Brentano, *The Origin of Our Knowledge of Right and Wrong* (*OKRW*), Roderick M. Chisholm and Elizabeth Schneewind, trans. (Humanities, 1969), p. 18. The German word that Chisholm and Schneewind translate as 'correct' is '*richtig*'.

2 Franz Brentano, *The Foundation and Construction of Ethics* (*F&C*), Elizabeth Schneewind, trans. (Humanities, 1973), p. 131.

3 Franz Brentano, *The True and the Evident* (*TE*), Roderick Chisholm, Ilse Politzer, and Kurt Fischer, trans. (Humanities, 1966), pp. 21 and 22.

4 *OKRW*, p. 26. Ewing's analysis of moral terms in *The Definition of Good* (Routledge & Kegan Paul, 1948) is very similar to Brentano's. Ewing defines 'good' as "what ought to be the object of a pro-attitude" (pp. 148–149). He goes on to define 'morally ought' as follows:

"'*A* morally ought to do this' means (1) it would be fitting for *A* to do this and (2) if he does not do it it is fitting that he should be an object of disapproval, or perhaps simply (2) without (1)" (p. 168).

Also see J. O. Urmson, *The Emotive Theory of Ethics* (Oxford, 1968), pp. 58–59.

"'This is good' is more like 'it is correct (in a sense of 'correct' which is opposed to 'mistaken') to approve of this' ... 'good' seems to resemble 'correctly to be approved of'."

Cf. C. D. Broad, 'Some Reflections on Moral Sense Theories in Ethics', in *Broad's Critical Essays in Moral Philosophy*, David Cheney, ed. (Humanities, 1971), esp. p. 194; and Broad's *Five Types of Ethical Theory* (Routledge & Kegan Paul, 1930), p. 283.

5 Carl Wellman, 'Emotivism and Ethical Objectivity', in Hospers and Sellars, eds., *Readings in Ethical Theory*, second edition (Prentice-Hall, 1970), p. 286.

6 Henry Sidgwick, *The Methods of Ethics* (Dover, 1966), pp. 26–27. Blanshard notes this passage with approval in *Reason and Goodness* (Allen and Unwin, 1961), p. 93. Cf. Gilbert Harman, *The Nature of Morality*

(Oxford, 1977), p. 42; W. D. Ross, *Foundations of Ethics* (Oxford, 1939), pp. 40–41; Bertrand Russell, 'A Reply to My Critics', in *The Philosophy of Bertrand Russell*, P. A. Schilpp, ed. (Tudor, 1944), p. 724; Vincent Tomas, 'Ethical Disagreement and the Emotive Theory of Values', *Mind 60*, 1950; Stephen Toulmin, *Reason in Ethics* (Cambridge, 1970), p. 71; and Charles L. Stevenson, *Ethics and Language* (Yale, 1944), p. 107.

[7] *OKRW*, p. 16: "... *Lieben oder hassen oder (wie man ebenso richtig ausdrücken könnte) ein Gefallen or Missfallen.*"

[8] *OKRW*, pp. 150–151, and *F&C*, p. 200.

[9] pp. 246 and 251.

[10] *TE*, pp. 109–110.

[11] *TE*, pp. 2–24.

[12] "It is self-contradictory to say that it would be morally better to choose a lesser good over a greater. ... No one can appeal to the disrepute of the dictum that the end justifies the means, for it deserves to be condemned only when it is used with reference to a certain end without regard to all the circumstances or to the consequences that would flow from its realization" (*F&C*, pp. 81 and 82). "By 'the right end' is meant the greatest degree of good and the greatest possible freedom from evil that are attainable under given circumstances" (*F&C*, p. 88). Also see *OKRW*, pp. 32 and 117.

[13] W. H. F. Barnes, 'A Suggestion About Value', in Hospers and Sellars, *op. cit.*, p. 241.

[14] A. J. Ayer, *Language, Truth and Logic* (Dover, 1952), p. 108.

[15] *Ethics and Language*, *op. cit.*, pp. 21–24 and 'The Emotive Meaning of Ethical Terms', in Hospers and Sellars, *op. cit.*, p. 262. In the latter passage, Stevenson says that when the word 'good' is used in the moral sense, one is making a statement about one's "moral approval", which is supposed to be stronger than ordinary approval.

[16] For example, Ross, *op. cit.*, Tomas, *op. cit.*, and Fred Feldman, *Introductory Ethics* (Prentice Hall, 1978), pp. 219–220.

[17] Stevenson says that an ethical disagreement consists in a disagreement "in interest" or a disagreement "in attitude". 'The Emotive Meaning of Ethical Terms', p. 263. Two people may be said to have a disagreement in interest or attitude when they have opposed attitudes about something and each is attempting to alter the other's attitude. Also see, *Ethics and Language*, pp. 3–4.

[18] Stevenson himself claims this. 'The Emotive Meaning of Ethical Terms', p. 262.

[19] p. 33.

[20] Cf. Tomas, *op. cit.*, page 215, and Brandt, *op. cit.*, p. 226.

[21] Cf. Tomas.

[22] R. M. Hare, *The Language of Morals* (Oxford, 1952); *Freedom and*

Reason (Oxford, 1963); and *Moral Thinking* (Oxford, 1981).

[23] *Language of Morals*, pp. 175–179.

[24] *Freedom and Reason*, p. 11.

[25] *Freedom and Reason*, p. 168, and *Moral Thinking*, pp. 58–59. Cf. Foot, 'Moral Beliefs', in *Theories of Ethics*, Foot, ed. (Oxford, 1967), p. 85.

[26] *Freedom and Reason*, p. 79, and *Moral Thinking*, p. 57–58.

[27] Stevenson analyzes such cases in this way, *Ethics and Language*, pp. 16–17.

[28] From Richard's opening monologue in Shakespeare's *Richard III*: "And therefore, – since I cannot prove a lover, I am determined to prove a villain . . .".

Note also the following song from the Musical 'Peter Pan':

"At last I've reached me Peak!
Peter killed and all the boys about to walk the plank
Ha, ha, ha!
I'm the greatest villain of all time!
Who is bluebeard?
(ans.) Nobody!
Who is Nero?
(ans.) Nobody!
Who is Jack the Ripper?
(ans.) Nobody!
Ha, ha, ha!
Who's the swiniest swine in the world?
(ans.) Captain Hook, Captain Hook
Who's the dirtiest dog in this wonderful world?
(ans.) Captain Hook, Captain Hook
Captain of villainy, murder and loot, eager to kill any
who says that his hook isn't cute. . . ."

It might be objected that the Captain's primary motive is not the love of evil, but a desire to distinguish himself or excel in some area. Hook surely does have a desire to excel, but this is compatible with the view that he loves evil for its own sake. Perhaps he has come to love evil for its own sake as *result* of having pursued it for the sake of distinction – just as we often come to attach intrinsic value to things such as money as a result of pursuing them for the sake of something else.

[29] 'The Emotive Meaning of Ethical Terms', p. 259.

[30] Warnock states this objection in a particularly forceful way. See, *Contemporary Moral Philosophy* (Macmillan, 1967), pp. 15–16.

[31] Cf. G. J. Warnock, *The Object of Morality* (Methuen, 1971):

"the 'general object' of morality, appreciation of which may enable us to *understand* the basis of moral evaluation, is to contribute to the betterment — or non-deterioration — of the human predicament, primarily and essentially by seeking to countervail 'limited sympathies' and their potentially most damaging effects" (p. 26).

[32] G. E. Moore, *Principia Ethica* (Cambridge, 1903).

[33] 'Does Moral Philosophy Rest on a Mistake?', in *Moral Obligation* (Oxford, 1968).

[34] Brentano says that it does not make sense to ask whether it is reasonable to do what is right (pursue the right end), *F&C*, p. 102.

[35] Also see R. W. Beardsmore, *Moral Reasoning* (Routledge & Kegan Paul, 1969).

[36] 'Moral Beliefs', p. 91.

[37] 'Moral Arguments', in *Virtues and Vices* (California, 1978), p. 100.

[38] R. M. Hare's *The Language of Morals*, pp. 148—149 (The Clarendon Press, Oxford, 1952); reproduced by the kind permission of R. M. Hare and Oxford University Press.

[39] 'Moral Beliefs', p. 95.

[40] Cf. Hare, *Moral Thinking*, pp. 17, and 73—74.

[41] *F&C*, p. 134.

[42] Nietzsche is well known for his view that there are no moral facts and that morality is an illusion. [*Twilight of the Idols*, in *The Portable Nietzsche*, Walter Kaufmann, trans. (Viking, 1968), p. 501; also see *The Will to Power*, Kaufmann and Hollingdale, trans. (Vintage, 1968), pp. 149 and 413, and *Beyond Good and Evil*, Marianne Cowan, trans. (Regnery, 1955), p. 76.] Nietzsche rejects morality and its notions of good and evil, guilt, retribution and moral praiseworthiness and blameworthiness. [*The Gay Science*, Kaufmann, trans. (Vintage, 1974), p. 216; *Thus Spoke Zarathustra*, in *The Portable Nietzsche*, pp. 150, 206, and 211; *The Will to Power*, pp. 134—136, and 528; and *On the Genealogy of Morals*, in *On the Genealogy of Morals and Ecce Homo*, Kaufmann and Hollingdale, trans. (Vintage, 1967), p. 129.] Nietzsche's own normative view only retains the notions of good and bad: "assuming it has long since been abundantly clear what my *aim* is, what the aim of that dangerous slogan is that is inscribed at the head of my last book *Beyond Good and Evil*. — At least this does not mean 'Beyond Good and Bad'." (Page 55, *Genealogy of Morals*.)

[43] J. L. Mackie, 'The Refutation of Morals', *Australasian Journal of Philosophy* (1946), and *Ethics* (Penguin, 1978), Chapter I. Cf. Paul Edwards, *The Logic of Moral Discourse* (Free Press, 1955), Chapter III; Richard Henson, 'Relativism and a Paradox About Meaning', *Philosophical Quarterly 11* (1961), p. 252; Richard Robinson, 'The Emotive Theory of Ethics', *Proceedings of the Aristotelian Society, Supplementary Volume 22* (1948), pp. 79—108.

Also see Westermarck, *Ethical Relativity* (Greenwood, 1970), pp. 45–47, and 60; and Friedrich Nietzsche, *Twilight of the Idols*, in the *Portable Nietzsche*, Kaufmann, ed. (Viking, 1954).

"My demand upon the philosopher is known, that he take his stand beyond good and evil and leave the illusion of moral judgment *beneath* himself. This demand follows from an insight which I was the first to formulate: that *there are altogether no moral facts*. Moral judgments agree with religious ones in believing in realities which are no realities. Morality is merely an interpretation of certain phenomena – more precisely, a misinterpretation" (p. 501).

CHAPTER TWO

[1] See Ewing, "Certain characteristics are such that the fitting response to whatever possesses them is a pro-attitude, and that is all there is to it" (*The Definition of Good*, p. 172). Also see Brentano *The Origin of Our Knowledge of Right and Wrong*, pp. 22–24, 84, 114, and 147; and C. D. Broad, *Five Types of Ethical Theory* (Routledge & Kegan-Paul, 1930), p. 283.

[2] Cf. Robert Coburn, 'Morality, Truth, and Relativism', *Ethics 92*, July, 1982.

[3] 'Ethical Absolutism and the Ideal Observer', in *Readings in Ethical Theory*, second ed., Hospers and Sellars, eds. (Prentice-Hall, 1970), p. 208.

[4] Cf. Firth, p. 207.

[5] Firth, pp. 212–221.

[6] Brandt calls his theory "the qualified attitude method". He reserves the term 'ideal observer theory' for those theories, such as Firth's, that define the meaning of moral concepts in terms of the notion of an ideal observer (*Ethical Theory*, p. 259).

D. D. Raphael sides with Brandt in rejecting the IOT as an analysis of the meaning of moral terms.

"Professor Firth proposes his ideal observer theory as an analysis of the *meaning* of moral judgments, and as such it is surely incredible. The suggestion is that when you or I say that an action is right, we mean, we intend to assert, that it would evoke a favorable reaction in a hypothetical observer who was omniscient, omnipercipient, disinterested, and dispassionate. We have all been making moral judgments happily – or unhappily – from early youth, but it is a safe bet that none of us had the remotest thought of connecting them with an omniscient and dispassionate observer until we heard of Professor Firth and his theory" ('The Impartial Spectator', *Proceedings of the British Academy*, 1972, p. 19).

I agree with Brandt and Raphael that the IOT is not a correct account of the meaning of moral judgments and concepts. I think that the Brentanist Theory constitutes a more plausible account of the meaning of moral terms than the IOT. (See Chapter One and Section 2.3.8.) However, I think that Raphael's criticisms fail to do justice to Firth's view. For all that Raphael has shown, the notion of an ideal observer could still be *implicit* in our ordinary moral notions, even though it is a notion that is unfamiliar to most people. Firth offers strong reasons for supposing that this is so (see p. 211).

[7] *Ethical Theory*, pp. 249–251.

[8] The notions of extreme and moderate relativism employed here are taken from Chapter 11 of *Ethical Theory*.

[9] *Mind* **48**, 1939.

[10] 'Ethical Relativity', p. 41.

[11] *Ibid*, p. 43.

[12] Hostility for *others* is ruled out by the requirement of dispassionateness. However, the sort of free-floating hostility that tends to be vented indiscriminately on everyone is not ruled out. Firth considers a stronger reading of the dispassionateness of the ideal observer — that he has no emotions at all. He rejects this interpretation on the grounds that the ethically significant reactions of the ideal observer (favorable and unfavorable attitudes about things that have a kind of "demand quality") have an essential emotional character. He suggests the following instead: an ideal observer has no emotions except for his ethically significant reactions (p. 217). It is unclear whether Firth intends this as a definite requirement or merely a suggestion for consideration. In any case, I think that this makes his conception of the ideal observer psychologically incoherent. No human being could have ethically significant feelings of demand and no other emotions. If one didn't have any other emotions, then one wouldn't have feelings of demand. If we allow any kind of favorable or unfavorable emotion to count as an ethically significant reaction (I am inclined to this view myself) then this condition does not rule the possibility that an ideal observer could displace hostility in his views and attitudes about moral questions.

[13] Cf. André Gorz, *The Traitor*, Richard Howard, trans. (Calder, 1960); and R. M. Hare, *Freedom and Reason* (Oxford, 1963), Chapters 9 and 11.

[14] Firth, 'Ethical Absolutism and the Ideal Observer', pp. 212–213.

[15] 'The Definition of an "Ideal Observer" in Ethics', *Philosophy and Phenomenological Research 15*, 1954, p. 410.

[16] Roderick Firth, 'Reply to Professor Brandt', *Philosophy and Phenomenological Research 15*, 1954, p. 417.

[17] *Ibid*.

[18] *Op. cit.*, p. 418.

[19] I believe that this solution to Firth's problem is preferable to the one

proposed by Brandt in 'Some Comments on Professor Firth's Reply', *Philosophy and Phenomenological Research 15*, 1954, pp. 422–423.

[20] Most people find it unbearable even to observe the suffering of people in war, much less adequately represent it to themselves. It requires an act of will not to avert one's eyes to the suffering of people in times of war and a further act of will to bring that suffering vividly to mind. I recall reading a statement by Lt. William Calley who said that, given the opportunity, he could produce an effective anti-war film which would instill a hatred of war in its viewers by depicting the horrors of war so graphically that the audience would be caused to vomit. (I might add here that consideration of this statement was largely responsible for my initial attraction to the IOT.)

Reflection on these matters weighs against those critics of utilitarianism who claim that the *number* of individuals affected by an action is irrelevant to its moral status. (Cf. John Taurek, 'Should the Numbers Count?', *Philosophy & Public Affairs 7*, 1977, pp. 293–316.) Such critics claim, for example, that killing 1000 people is not preferable to killing 1000000 people. Given that we cannot adequately represent this difference, it is not surprising that we do not consider it to be morally relevant. I rather suspect that we would think this difference to be morally relevant if we could adequately represent it to ourselves.

[21] Hare, *Moral Thinking*, p. 99. These lines are taken from Blake's 'On Another's Sorrow', in *Songs of Innocence and Experience*.

[22] The account of 'emotional infection' given here follows that of Max Scheler in Chapters Two and Three of *The Nature of Sympathy*, trans. by Peter Heath (Archon Books, 1973).

[23] David Hume, *A Treatise of Human Nature* (Oxford, 1888), p. 317. Cf. Adam Smith, *The Theory of Moral Sentiments* (Oxford, 1974), p. 28. According to Schopenhauer, compassion involves "immediate participation in the suffering of others". We experience the other creature's suffering ourselves, but we do not lose sight of our own individuality. We suffer "in" his person. Schopenhauer claims that the welfare and ill-fare of others cannot move us to action or become "an ultimate object of our will" unless it is directly experienced in this way. *On the Basis of Morality*, trans. by E. F. J. Payne (Bobbs Merrill, 1965), pp. 143–147. Cf. Edith Stein, *The Problem of Empathy*, trans. by Waltraut Stein (Martinus Nijhoff, 1970), p. 14.

[24] The account of sympathy given here is similar to the one presented by C. M. Mercer in *Sympathy and Ethics* (Oxford, 1972), pp. 7–10 and 17. According to Mercer, sympathy involves (1) fellow feeling, and (2) concern for the welfare of the other person (creature). Fellow feeling involves knowing or understanding the feelings of others. It is not clear whether Mercer would require occurrently representing the feelings of others, although he

stresses that sympathizing with another person does not require that one undergo the same kinds of experiences oneself.

[25] Cf. Smith, p. 24, and Franz Brentano, *The Foundation and Construction of Ethics*, trans. by Elizabeth Schneewind (Humanities, 1973), p. 92.

[26] This is something that I know from my own personal experience. I was 24 years old before I ever experienced extreme physical pain and my previous representations of such pain were grossly inadequate.

[27] In his most recent book, *A Theory of the Good and the Right* (Oxford, 1979), Brandt devotes a great deal of attention to the question of when desires and aversions can be said to be rational. He considers desires and aversions based on one's having had false beliefs to be irrational (pp. 115—116). However, his reasons for discounting such desires are different from those that I have proposed here. According to Brandt, desires that one has as a result of having had false beliefs in the past are irrational because they would be extinguished by "cognitive psychotherapy" (p. 113). To subject a desire to cognitive psychotherapy is to confront it with a vivid and prolonged awareness of all of the relevant facts about the nature of its object. A desire or aversion is rational if and only if it would withstand cognitive psychotherapy. I believe that my way of discounting desires based on false beliefs is preferable to Brandt's. Accepting Brandt's view requires an unwarranted degree of faith in the causal efficacy of cognitive psychotherapy. Brandt gives us no reasons to suppose that cognitive psychotherapy can always extinguish desires that are based upon false beliefs or incomplete information. He is committed to the view that a desire that persists in the light of cognitive psychotherapy must count as a rational desire, even if one's having the desire is dependent on one's having *had* false beliefs about the nature of its object in the past.

One advantage of Brandt's approach over my own is that it allows for a greater measure of knowledge concerning moral questions. Given Brandt's view, we can sometimes know that a certain desire or attitude is correct or incorrect by determining whether or not it would persist in the light of cognitive psychotherapy. One can determine this by subjecting the desire to cognitive psychotherapy — or at least as close an approximation of it as is possible. (Cognitive psychotherapy is an ideal notion, because, for all practical purposes, it is impossible to know that one has represented vividly all of the relevant facts about something.) On the other hand, my view makes it extremely difficult to tell what is the correct attitude to have about something. For it is very difficult to tell what sorts of attitudes it would be possible to have about something if one had never had any false beliefs about it. Such judgments involve counter-factual claims of an extremely complicated sort, e.g., if someone had not had false beliefs x and y and if he had all of the relevant facts about _____ vividly to mind, then he could not fail to have had such and such an attitude about _____. Such counter-factuals are much too complicated for us to be certain of what exactly is the correct view about any given issue.

To this objection I offer the following two replies. First, given the extent to which our attitudes depend on our being or having been misinformed, and given the great difficulty involved in saying what our attitudes would have been if we had not been misinformed, our claims to moral knowledge are considerably weakened. For all that we know many of the views and attitudes that we take to be most certain might be dependent on our being or having been misinformed, in which case we cannot know for certain that these beliefs and attitudes are correct. Second, my view still permits us to say that there are many cases in which the rough outlines of the correct view can be known with reasonable certainty. My theory does not enable us to determine a precise code for sexual morality. Among other things, it is virtually impossible to tell whether all ideal observers would agree in not having an unfavorable attitude about prostitution and sado-masochism. On the other hand, it seems reasonable to suppose that there are some forms of extra-marital and homosexual sexual activities that no ideal observer would have an unfavorable attitude about. (From this we can conclude that it is objectively true that such activities are morally permissible.) Further it seems quite certain that there are many forms of extra-marital and homo-sexual relationships that are such that they would not be viewed with great disfavor by all ideal observers. (All ideal observers would not have the kinds of extremely unfavorable attitudes that characterize those who view such relations as great moral evils.) It follows that it is not objectively true that all forms of homosexual and extra-marital sexual relations are great moral evils.

[28] Max Scheler, *Ressentiment*, trans. by William Holdheim (New York: Schoken Books, 1972), pp. 39–40. The literal root meaning of the French word '*ressentiment*' is '*re*feeling. or 'feeling again'.

[29] *Ressentiment*, p. 47.

[30] Scheler says that *ressentiment* perverts or distorts our consciousness of an eternal and objective realm of values (*Ressentiment*, p. 73). I think it very doubtful that there are any such entities as objective values. Belief in objective values is also contrary to the spirit of the ideal observer theory. Objective values are presumably entities that make it the case that certain moral judgments are correct or incorrect. On the other hand, the ideal observer theory claims that the correctness of a moral judgment about something is determined by the reactions that an ideal observer would have to it. I will attempt to provide a rationale for discounting moral judgments that are expressions of *ressentiment* that does not presuppose the existence of objective values.

[31] For example, the rage vented by those who say that we ought to "Nuke Iran" was not for the most part evoked by anything the Iranians have done. Rather, it is a free-floating anger which finds a convenient outlet in such judgments.

[32] It might be argued that emotional displacement is effectively ruled out by the requirement of full information. An emotion aroused by x cannot be displaced on y, unless one is ignorant of the fact that x originally caused the emotion. An ideal observer who was fully informed about the causes of his own emotions and attitudes could not displace emotions. However, this is very doubtful. For there seem to be many cases in which people knowingly displace emotions. For example someone may "let off steam" built up from other sources by venting his rage at an umpire during a baseball game. While it may be both rational and therapeutic to displace emotions in this way, hostile attitudes for umpires and other consciously chosen scapegoats are inappropriate or incorrect. This is a case in which it is rational for one to bring it about that one has an inappropriate attitude about something.

[33] Cf. Nietzsche, *On the Genealogy of Morals*, in *On the Genealogy of Morals and Ecce Homo*, trans. by Walter Kaufmann and R. J. Hollingdale (Vintage Books, 1967).

"Weakness is being lied into something *meritorious* . . . and impotence which does not requite into 'goodness of heart'; anxious lowliness into 'humility'; subjection to those one hates into 'obedience' . . . . The inoffensiveness of the weak man, even the cowardice of which he has so much, his lingering at the door, his being ineluctably compelled to wait, here acquire flattering names, such as 'patience,' and are even called virtue itself; his inability for revenge is called unwillingness to revenge, perhaps even forgiveness ('for *they* know not what they do — we alone know what *they* do!') They also speak of 'loving one's enemies' and sweat as they do." (p. 47; also see *GM*, p. 46 and *The Will to Power*, Hollingdale and Kaufmann, trans. (Vintage, 1968), pp. 183, 196 and 398.)

[34] At some level the person who takes a sour grapes attitude about something knows that he really wants it. However, his knowledge is far from being clear, unconfused, or present to mind.

[35] Cf. W. D. Falk, 'Hume on Is/Ought', *Canadian Journal of Philosophy 6*, 1975, p. 375.

[36] Firth, p. 211.

[37] Cf. Hume, *Enquiry Concerning the Principles of Morals* (Oxford, 1902).

"When a man denominates another his *enemy*, his *rival*, his *antagonist*, his *adversary*, he is understood to speak the language of self-love, and to express sentiments, peculiar to himself, and arising from his particular circumstances and situation. But when he bestows on any man the epithets of *vicious* or *odious* or *depraved*, he then speaks another language, and expresses sentiments, in which he expects all his audience are to concur with him. He must here, therefore depart from his private and particular situation, and must choose a point of view, common to him with others (p. 272).

[38] Firth has related this to me in private conversation.

[39] As well as I am able to determine, Hume holds that moral judgments involve claims about the attitudes (as opposed to the judgments) of ideal observers. So, Hume would presumably hold (II) (or something like (II)) rather than (I). Adam Smith's views are much more difficult to classify.

In the *Treatise*, Hume says that when we call someone virtuous or vicious, we simply mean that the contemplation of his character (from an impartial perspective) causes one to feel approbation or disapprobation (pp. 469 and 471–472). In the *Enquiry*, Hume defines virtue to be "*Whatever mental action or quality gives to a spectator the pleasing sentiment of approbation*; and vice the contrary" (p. 289). He goes on to add that the spectator must have a full knowledge of all of the relevant facts and circumstances (p. 290).

Smith's version of the IOT is presented in *The Theory of Moral Sentiments* (Oxford, 1974). The ideal spectator is defined as knowing all of the relevant facts. He must be able to imagine all of the circumstances of those about whom he makes his judgments down to the minutest details (p. 21). The spectator must also be impartial. By this, Smith means that his own personal interests are not involved in the situations about which he makes his judgments. One cannot be an ideal spectator about any issue concerning which one has a personal interest. To my knowledge, Smith does not give a clear statement of the place of the notion of the ideal spectator within his theory. In the second edition of *The Theory of Moral Sentiments*, he says that we use the concept of an ideal spectator to make judgments about our own conduct. We approve or disapprove of our own conduct depending on whether we think that an impartial spectator would approve or disapprove of it (pp. 109–110). Smith's notions of approval and disapproval are not sufficiently clear for me to determine whether he accepts a judgment or attitude version of the IOT. He often identifies the impartial spectator with conscience or "the man within the breast". Raphael thinks that only in the later sixth edition of *The Theory of Moral Sentiments* did the idea of the impartial spectator serve as the ultimate general standard for moral judgments. See Raphael, 'The Impartial Spectator', *op. cit.*, Raphael's introduction to *The Theory of Moral Sentiments*, and *The Theory of Moral Sentiments*, p. 294.

[40] There is an excellent scene in the film 'Mirage' in which Gregory Peck discovers the body of an innocent man brutally murdered by agents of a sinister organization headed by a man known as "The Major". The heroine,

Diane Baker, who is the Major's disenchanted lover, remains with the organization out of fear. Peck forces an unwilling Baker to view the man's corpse and does not permit her to avert her eyes from the bloody sight. After this, she gains the courage and determination to fight the Major.

41 In this context, I think that it would also be helpful to note how very atypical approval of genocide is even among people who aren't ideal observers. It is important to remember that genocide was never a *public policy* of the Nazi party. The Nazi leaders realized that such policies would be abhorrent to the vast majority of the German people. Finally, we should also note that few present day Nazis in the United States *profess* approval of genocide. They claim rather that the holocaust never occurred. See, for example, A. R. Butz, *The Hoax of the Twentieth Century* (Historical Review Press, 1976). Similarly, many present-day Stalinists deny that Stalin was a mass-murderer. This is a perverse reading of history, but it is not the kind of utter repudiation of conventional values that it is often made out to be.

42 Brandt also suggests that the IOT can be used as a criterion for the correctness of an individual person's moral judgments ('The Definition of an "Ideal Observer" in Ethics', p. 408). Cf. Gilbert Harman, *The Nature of Morality* (Oxford, 1977), Ch. IV.

43 Cf. Smith, *Theory of Moral Sentiments*, pp. 139–140; Brentano, *The Origin of Our Knowledge of Right and Wrong*, pp. 135–136; and Thomas Carson, 'Happiness, Contentment, and the Good Life', *Pacific Philosophical Quarterly* **62**, October 1981.

44 *Principia Ethica*, Chapter I.

45 W. D. Ross, *The Right and the Good* (Oxford, 1930), p. 28.

46 Ewing, *op. cit.*, pp. 146-149 and 168–172. For references to Brentano supporting this interpretation see Chapter One.

CHAPTER THREE

1 Frederick Olafson, in 'Meta-Ethics and the Moral Life', *Philosophical Review 65* (1956) and B. C. Postow, in 'Dishonest Relativism', *Analysis 39* (1979) defend views of this sort. However, the arguments that they offer, particularly Postow's, are different from those that I will offer in this chapter.

2 Brandt suggests that all disagreements about moral questions might cease if the parties to the disagreements could agree about all of the relevant facts. See 'The Significance of Differences of Ethical Opinion for Ethical Rationalism', *Philosophy and Phenomenological Research 4* (1944), p. 482; also see Brandt's article 'Ethical Relativism', in *The Encyclopedia of Philosophy*, Paul Edwards, editor (Macmillan, 1967), and Karl Duncker, 'Ethical Relativity?', *Mind 48* (1939), pp. 39–53.

[3] Kant comes to mind as a possible exception. Unlike most other philosophers he does not think that the moral status of such things as lying and making promises in bad faith is relative to the situation in which they are performed — according to Kant it is always wrong to lie or make promises in bad faith. But even Kant would say that there are certian kinds of acts, e.g., harming others, whose rightness or wrongness depends on the situation in which they are performed. Whether or not it is right to do something that will harm another person depends on the circumstances of the act.

[4] My use of the term 'normative relativism' (as opposed to 'meta-ethical relativism') is in accordance with the standard terminology. Cf. William Frankena, *Ethics*, second ed. (Prentice-Hall, 1973), p. 109; Richard Brandt, 'Ethical Relativism', in *The Encyclopedia of Philosophy* (Macmillan, 1967); Gilbert Harman, 'What Is Moral Relativism?', in *Values and Morals*, A. I. Goldman and J. Kim, eds. (Reidel, 1978); and Paul Taylor, *Problems of Moral Philosophy* (Dickenson, 1967), pp. 44–47.

[5] Richard Brandt, *Ethical Theory* (Prentice Hall, 1959), p. 272, cf. p. 154; Brandt, *Hopi Ethics* (Chicago, 1954), p. 235; and Brandt, 'Ethical Relativism', *op. cit.*, p. 75.

[6] 'Social Science and Ethical Relativism', in *Ethical Relativism*, John Ladd, editor (Wadsworth, 1973), p. 96.

[7] 'What Is Moral Relativism?', in *Values and Morals*, A. I. Goldman and J. Kim, eds. (Reidel, 1978), p. 146.

[8] In his introduction to *Ethical Relativism*, Ladd defines 'ethical relativism' as follows:

"If we try to formulate the doctrine of ethical relativism in more abstract terms, we find two possible versions, a negative one and an affirmative one. The negative version is that there are no universally valid moral principles (or moral codes); the positive version is that every moral principle (or moral code) is equally valid" (p. 8).

Carl Wellman offers the following definition in *Morals and Ethics* (Scott Foresman, 1975): "What the relativist is asserting is that moral judgers may disagree without error, that one judgment may be legitimate for one judger while a contrary judgment may be equally legitimate for another" (p. 291). Also see Frankena, *op. cit.*, p. 109, Kai Nielsen, 'Ethical Relativism and the Facts of Cultural Relativity', in *Understanding Moral Philosophy*, James Rachels, editor (Dickenson, 1976), p. 18; Nielsen, 'Anthropology and Ethics', *Journal of Value Inquiry* 5 (1971), p. 261; Abraham Edel, *Ethical Judgment* (Free Press, 1955), p. 30; D. H. Munro, *Empiricism and Ethics* (Cambridge, 1967), p. 122; T. L. McClintock, 'The Argument for Ethical Relativism from the Diversity of Morals', *Monist* 47, 1963, p. 530; B. C. Postow, *op. cit.*;

Morris Ginzberg, *On the Diversity of Morals* (Macmillan, 1956), p. 100; and Frank Hartung, 'Cultural Relativity and Moral Judgments', *Philosophy of Science 21* (1954), p. 118. Cf. Karl R. Popper, *The Open Society and Its Enemies*, fifth ed. (Princeton, 1971), Volume II, p. 387. "If two parties disagree, this may mean that one is wrong, or the other, or both: this is the view of the criticist. It does not mean, as the relativist will have it that both may be equally correct." Westermarck holds that a moral judgment is true iff the individual making the judgment actually experiences the "moral approval" or "disapproval", i.e., disinterested approval or disapproval, that he expresses in making his judgment (p. 141). Since it is possible for an individual to experience moral approval concerning something about which someone else experiences moral disapproval, Westermarck's theory (which he describes as a version of "ethical relativism") implies that conflicting moral judgments can both be true. (*Ethical Relativity*, Greenwood, 1970). Parts of Plato's *Theatetus* are given to a discussion of Protagoras' view "that what seems true to anyone is true for him to whom it seems so" (170a: see also 166d). This is a theory about the status of *all* beliefs and, as such, it is a much more general view than ethical relativism. The Protagorean view, however, entails ethical relativism as it is defined here. It implies that if you and I have conflicting beliefs, *b* and *b'* about a moral issue, *m*, then *b* is true for you and *b'* is true for me. This would seem to imply that there is no moral judgment about *m* that is more correct than all other conflicting judgments. For *b* and *b'* are equally correct and since, according to Protagoras, no beliefs are objectively correct, there is no belief about *m* that is more correct than either *b* or *b'*. Socrates attacks Protagorean subjectivism on the grounds that it leads to the following two absurd consequences: (i) that no one ever has false beliefs (170c), and thus that (ii) no man (including Protagoras who claims to be a teacher) can ever be said to be wiser or more knowledgeable than another (171d).

[9] Cf. Brentano, *The True and the Evident*, Roderick Chisholm, Ilse Politzer, and Kurt Fischer, trans. (Humanities, 1966), p. 85: "Everyone who believes or rejects something, believes of himself that he believes or rejects correctly; if he did not believe this of himself, he would not be judging at all".

[10] Cf. Antony Duff, 'Desire, Duty, and Moral Absolutes', *Philosophy 55*, 1980, p. 229.

[11] Cf. J. O. Urmson, *The Emotive Theory of Ethics* (Oxford, 1968), "'This is good' is more like 'it is correct (in a sense of 'correct' which is opposed to 'mistaken') to approve of this' . . . 'good' seems to resemble 'correctly to be approved of'" (pp. 58–59); Franz Brentano, *The Origin of Our Knowledge of Right and Wrong*, Roderick M. Chisholm and Elizabeth Schneewind, trans. (Humanities, 1969). "We call a thing *good* when love relating to it is correct. In the broadest sense of the term, the good is that which is worthy of love,

that which can be loved with a love that is correct" (p. 18). Cf. Brentano, *The Foundation and Construction of Ethics*, Elizabeth Schneewind, trans. (Humanities, 1973), pp. 131–134; David Hume, *Inquiry Concerning the Principles of Morals* (Oxford, 1902), p. 272; Henry Sidgwick, *The Methods of Ethics* (Dover, 1966), pp. 26–27; Charles Stevenson, *Ethics and Language* (Yale, 1944), p. 107; Bertrand Russell, 'A Reply to My Critics', in *The Philosophy of Bertrand Russell*, Schilpp, ed. (Tudor, 1944), p. 724; Fredrick Olafson, 'Meta-ethics and the Moral Life', *Philosophical Review 65*, (1956); Carl Wellman, 'Emotivism and Ethical Objectivity', in Hospers and Sellars, *Readings in Ethical Theory*, 2nd ed. (Prentice-Hall, 1970), p. 286; A. C. Ewing, 'A Suggested Non-Naturalistic Analysis of Good', in Hospers and Sellars, *op. cit.*, p. 129; W. D. Ross, *Foundations of Ethics* (Oxford, 1939), pp. 34, 41, and 261; Richard Brandt, *Ethical Theory*, p. 266; Gilbert Harman, *The Nature of Morality* (Oxford, 1977), p. 42; Maurice Mandelbaum, *The Phenomenology of Moral Experience*, (Johns Hopkins, 1969), pp. 42, 122, and 263; and Vincent Tomas, 'Ethical Disagreements and the Emotive Theory of Values', *Mind 60*, 1950, pp. 205–222.

[12] Thus R1 is an ultra-extreme version of meta-ethical relativism; it entails (D). (See Section 3.3.) Protagoras' view "that what seems true to anyone is true for him to whom it seems so", which Socrates criticizes in the *Theatetus* (170a, and 166d), entails R1. The Protagorean view is also criticized by Husserl in *The Logical Investigations*, trans. J. N. Findlay (Humanities, 1970), Volume I, pp. 135–146.

[13] (IV) is very similar to the view defended by Paul Taylor in *Normative Discourse* (Prentice-Hall, 1961). According to Taylor, value judgments can only be justified or validated by appeal to the ultimate principles of a given ethical system (p. 125). Ultimate moral principles cannot, themselves, be justified (p. 132). However, the choice of such principles can be "vindicated" or "pragmatically justified". We vindicate a system of ultimate norms by causing someone to decide that, upon reflection, the system is part of a way of life that he really wants to participate in (pp. 132, and 135). The only sense in which one can justify a way of life is to show that it would be rational to choose it (p. 157). It is rational for one to choose a way of life if and only if one would choose it if one's choice were: (a) "free" (i.e., not the result of physical or psychological compulsion, but a genuine preference); (b) "enlightened", i.e., based on full information about the features of various kinds of lives; and (c) "impartial" (among other things this means that the preference for a particular way of life can't just be based on the fact that one was brought up in that way of life) (pp. 165–170). It is virtually certain that different persons could be rational in choosing very different kinds of lives. Therefore, Taylor seems to be committed to some version of relativism. We can state the view to which Taylor is committed as follows:

a moral judgment is true for x if and only if it is consistent with the principles that are included in the way of life he would most prefer if he were fully rational.

14 A more rigorous argument for this claim can be stated as follows: *Assume,*

(1)   It is correct in a sense that is opposed to mistaken for S to accept a set of principles, p, i.e., it would be incorrect for him to accept any alternative set of principles instead.

(2)   It is correct in a sense that is opposed to mistaken for S to accept all of the moral judgments about actual and possible cases that p commits one to.

(To say that a principle p, 'commits one' to a judgment j, about a particular case c, is to say that the conjunction of p and the set of factual statements that describes c entails j.) (2) follows from (1). To say that (2) follows from (1) amounts to saying that the logical implications of what is true for one must also be true for one. Since p is true for S regardless of what moral principles he accepts, the implications of p must be true for S, regardless of what principles he accepts. Therefore, (1) implies the following:

(2′)   It is correct in a sense that is opposed to mistaken for S to accept all of the particular moral judgments that p commits one to, regardless of what moral principles he accepts.

(3)   For any moral principle, p, there is an alternative principle, p_1, such that some of the particular moral judgments about actual or hypothetical cases that it commits one to are inconsistent with those that p commits one to.

(4)   If it is correct (in a sense that is opposed to mistaken) for S to accept a particular moral judgment, i.e., if it is true for S that x (in some sense that is opposed to mistaken) it must be false for S that not-x.

Therefore,

(5)   It would be incorrect for S to accept some of the moral judgments that p_1 commits one to, even if he accepts p_1 (from (2′), (3), and (4)).

The foregoing argument shows that (IV) commits us to the view that it can never be correct (in a sense that is opposed to mistaken) for one to accept a particular set of moral principles as opposed to all other alternative principles. This is proven as follows: we assume that it can be correct (in a sense that is opposed to mistaken) for a person to accept a particular set of moral principles (premise 1); then, from (1) we derive (5), which is inconsistent with (IV).

[15] R. W. Beardsmore, one of the leading proponents of the views of the later Wittgenstein in moral philosophy, seems to be committed to something like (V) in his book *Moral Reasoning* (Routledge & Kegan Paul, 1969). Beardsmore claims that the meaning of moral terms and concepts is determined in part by the things to which they apply (p. 121). The intelligibility of our ordinary moral notions presupposes the existence of substantial agreement about the application and criteria for the application of these terms. [Cf. Wittgenstein, *Philosophical Investigations*, Anscombe, trans. (Macmillan, 1953), pp. 88 and 226; also see *On Certainty*, Anscombe and von Wright, trans. (Blackwell, 1969), p. 82.] There is no possibility of basic or fundamental disagreement over moral principles, because if two people have radically different criteria for calling something good they are using the word 'good' in different senses. They don't disagree, their views are simply unintelligible to each other (pp. 76 and 79). One's basic moral standards depend on the way of life to which one adheres (p. 130). Moral standards presuppose a social context — they must in some sense be accepted by society (pp. 130–131). The view to which Beardsmore seems to be committed is that a moral judgment is true for someone only if it is entailed by the principles of the group or form of life of which the person is a part. Cf. Melville J. Herskovits, *Man and His Works* (Alfred Knopf, 1967), p. 76 and *Cultural Relativism* (Random House, 1972), pp. 31 and 33. Herskovits claims that every set of norms is valid for the culture that embraces it.

[16] Postow, *op. cit.*

CHAPTER FOUR

[1] Cf. R. M. Hare 'Nothing Matters', in *The Meaning of Life*, Sanders and Cheney, eds. (Prentice-Hall, 1980), p. 100.

[2] This mode of life (making everything completely arbitrary) is recommended by *A* in 'The Rotation Method', in Volume I of Kierkegaard's *Either/Or*. The force of this example may be vitiated by the following considerations. The choice of which shoe to put on first is dependent on a prior choice to put one's shoes on and that choice is almost always the result of a desire or preference that one have one's shoes on.

[3] Many relativists such as Mackie hold that belief in the objectivity of morals is a result of 'objectifying values'. From the fact that we value something we (mistakenly) conclude that it must be valuable, i.e., have some objective

characteristics that command those attitudes. (See *Ethics* (Penguin, 1977), Chapter I.) Nietzsche and Sartre hold that belief in the objectivity of morals results from a desire to avoid responsibility for one's values — we prefer to think that our values and attitudes are not of our own choice and creation, but rather that they are commanded by the nature of things. (See *Existentialism and Human Emotions*, p. 23 and *The Will to Power*, p. 159.) This is a very important theme in existentialism. I will not attempt to assess the accuracy of this view about the genealogy of objectivist meta-ethical views. However, I should like to note that it seems somewhat confused for one to try to avoid responsibility for one's moral views by rejecting moral objectivism. There is no reason to fear assuming responsibility for one's own values unless there is some chance that they can be mistaken. Unless one accepts at least a weak version of objectivism there is no reason to fear taking responsibility for one's attitudes. Thus this fear should not be what causes one to accept objectivism — it doesn't make any sense to have the fear unless one first accepts objectivism.

4 An interesting question, which I will pose but not attempt to answer, is the following: 'can I feel guilty about something that I *know* that I am not responsible for?' For example, can I feel guilty about American slavery or our country's slaughter of the American Indians? The same question arises in the case of shame. Clearly guilt and shame involve some self-reference. The things about which one feels guilty or ashamed must be things that one identifies as somehow being 'one's own'. But it is not clear what can and cannot count as one's own.

5 Cf. Nietzsche, *On the Genealogy of Morals*, and G. E. M. Anscombe, 'Modern Moral Philosophy', in *Ethics*, Thomson and Dworkin, eds. (Harper and Row, 1968), pp. 185—187, 191, and 196.

6 According to Aristotle, the appetites or desires of a virtuous person must be in harmony with the dictates of reason. Therefore, the virtuous person does not need to go against his desires or inclinations in order to act correctly (*Nicomachean Ethics*, 1104b15—20).

7 According to Kant, actions in accordance with duty that are done from benevolence or any other "inclination" possess no moral worth. Only actions performed for duty's sake have moral worth. (*Groundwork of the Metaphysic of Morals*, H. J. Paton, trans. (Harper and Row, 1964), pp. 64—68 (G397—398)). Kant is committed to saying that a person who acts against his inclinations and desires in doing what is right because of a sense of duty is *more worthy* than someone who does his duty simply out of benevolence or love of humanity. I am not certain that Kant would hold that the sort of person who does his duty but needs to fight his instincts in order to do so is more worthy than the sort of person who acts dutifully and whose actions are overdetermined by both the sense of duty and inclination. (Richard Henson

argues that Kant is not committed to this view in his paper 'What Kant Might Have Said: Moral Worth and the Overdetermination of Dutiful Action', *The Philosophical Review 88*, 1979; Barbara Herman criticizes Henson in 'On the Value of Acting from the Motive of Duty', *Philosophical Review 90*, 1981.) However, there seem to be no grounds on which Kant could deny the claim that, for him, the sort of person who acts dutifully against his inclinations is at least as worthy as any other kind of person.

[8] Cf. E. P. Brandon, 'Subjectivism and Seriousness', *The Philosophical Quarterly* **30**, April 1980, p. 97 and Hastings Rashdall, *Is Conscience an Emotion?* (Unwin, 1914), p. 199.

[9] *The Object of Morality* (Methuen, 1971), p. 26.

[10] The distinction between "natural virtues" and "artificial virtues" is derived from Hume. For an illuminating discussion of these notions see, Marcia Baron, 'Hume's Noble Lie: An Account of His Artificial Virtues', *Canadian Journal of Philosophy 12*, pp. 539–555.

APPENDIX I

[1] All references are to the titles and page numbers of the works listed in the bibliography. Nietzsche also thinks that moral judgments can be an expression of hatred for the world as a whole; see *WP*, 253, 317 and 323, and *TI*, 87.

[2] *GS*, 216; *Z*, 150, 206, 211; *WP*, 134–36; *GM*, 129; and *HA*, Vol. I, 107.

[3] In the following passages, Nietzsche claims that the value of an individual is determined by his strength or weakness — strong people are good and weak people are bad: *AC*, 115; *GM*, 78; and *WP*, 33, 206, 349, 356, 378, and 457. There are numerous passages in which he identifies health with strength and sickness with weakness: *AC*, 132; *TI*, 56; *GM*, 143; and *GS*, 295. See Thomas Carson, 'The *Übermensch* and Nietzsche's Theory of Value', *International Studies in Philosophy 13*, 1981, pp. 9–30.

[4] See Carson, *op. cit.*

APPENDIX II

[1] Thoreau seems to be committed to (1). "The only obligation I have a right to assume is to do at any time what I think is right." ('Civil Disobedience', in *The American Tradition in Literature*, Bradley, Beatty and Long, eds. (Norton, 1967), p. 1463.)

[2] Few, if any, philosophers hold either (1) or (2). However, these views enjoy considerable popular acceptance. This is evidenced by the fact that it is common for people to reject moral criticisms of another person's conduct,

e.g., 'it was wrong for him to do that', by replying that the person believed that the act was right or that it was in accordance with his basic moral principles.

3 Socrates attributes something like (3) to Protagoras in the *Theatetus*: "I hold that whatever practices seem right and laudable to any particular state are so, for that state, so long as it holds by them" (167c). There are a considerable number of anthropologists who accept something like (3). See Ruth Benedict, 'Anthropology and the Abnormal', in *The Philosophy of Society*, Roger Beehle and Alan Dregson, eds. (Methuen, 1978), p. 286 (— according to Benedict to say that one's action is morally good simply means that it is approved of by the standards of one's society); W. G. Sumner, *Folkways* (Ginn and Co., 1907), pp. 28 and 521; and A. L. Kroeber, *Anthropology* (Harcourt Brace, 1948), p. 265.

4 (4) is often a matter of dispute in discussions about business ethics. Some people justify the actions of business firms which engage in bribery in foreign countries on the grounds that such practices are compatible with the moral codes of the societies in which they occur.

APPENDIX III

1 *Moral Thinking*, p. 6.

2 *Moral Thinking*, p. 46.

3 *Moral Thinking*, p. 55, ff.

4 *Moral Thinking*, pp. 89 and 109, and *Freedom and Reason*, Chapters 6 and 11.

5 *Freedom and Reason*, p. 79; and *Moral Thinking*, pp. 58–59.

6 *Freedom and Reason*, Chapter 11.

7 *Moral Thinking*, pp. 94–95.

8 *Moral Thinking*, p. 99.

SELECTED BIBLIOGRAPHY

(WORKS CITED)

Adel, Abraham: 1955, *Ethical Judgment*, Free Press, New York.

Anscombe, G. E. M.: 1968, 'Modern Moral Philosophy', in *Ethics* Thomson and Dworkin (eds.), Harper and Row, New York.

Aristotle: 1962, *Nicomachean Ethics*, Martin Ostwald (trans.), Bobbs-Merrill, Indianapolis.

Ayer, A. J.: 1952, *Language, Truth, and Logic*, Dover, New York.

Barnes, W. H. F.: 1970, 'A Suggestion About Value', in Hospers and Sellars.

Baron, Marcia: 1982, 'Hume's Noble Lie: An Account of His Artificial Virtues', *Canadian Journal of Philosophy* 12, pp. 539–555.

Beardsmore, R. W.: 1969, *Moral Reasoning*, Routledge & Kegan Paul, London.

Benedict, Ruth: 1978, 'Anthropology and the Abnormal', in *The Philosophy of Society*, Roger Beehle and Alan Dregson (eds.), Methuen, London.

Blake, William: 1946, 'On Another's Sorrow', in *Songs of Innocence and Experience*, in *The Portable Blake*, Alfred Kazin (ed.), Viking, New York.

Blanshard, Brand: 1961, *Reason and Goodness*, Allen and Unwin, London.

Brandon, E. P.: 1980, 'Subjectivism and Seriousness', *Philosophical Quarterly* 30, pp. 97–107.

Brandt, Richard: 1979, *A Theory of the Good and the Right*, The Clarendon Press, Oxford.

Brandt, Richard: 1967, 'Ethical Relativism', in *The Encyclopedia of Philosophy*, Paul Edwards (ed.), Macmillan, New York.

Brandt, Richard: 1959, *Ethical Theory*, Prentice-Hall, Engelwood Cliffs.

Brandt, Richard: 1954, *Hopi Ethics*, University of Chicago Press, Chicago.

Brandt, Richard: 1954, 'Some Comments on Professor Firth's Reply', *Philosophy and Phenomenological Research* 15, pp. 422–423.

Brandt, Richard: 1954, 'The Definition of an "Ideal Observer" in Ethics', *Philosophy and Phenomenological Research* 15, pp. 407–413.

Brandt, Richard: 1944, 'The Significance of Differences in Opinion for Ethical Rationalism', *Philosophy and Phenomenological Research* 4, pp. 469–495.

Brentano, Franz: 1973, *The Foundation and Construction of Ethics*

Elizabeth H. Schneewind (trans.), Humanities, New York.

Brentano, Franz: 1969, *The Origin of Our Knowledge of Right and Wrong*, Roderick M. Chisholm and Elizabeth H. Schneewind (trans.), Humanities, New York.

Brentano, Franz: 1966, *The True and the Evident*, Roderick M. Chisholm, Ilse Politzer, and Kurt Fischer (trans.), Humanities, New York.

Brinton, Crane: 1941, *Nietzsche*, Harvard University Press, Cambridge.

Broad, C. D.: 1930, *Five Types of Ethical Theory*, Routledge & Kegan Paul, London.

Broad, C. D.: 1971, 'Some Reflections on Moral Sense Theories in Ethics', in *Broad's Critical Essays in Moral Philosophy*, David Cheney (ed.), Humanities, New York.

Butz, A. R.: 1975, *The Hoax of the Twentieth Century*, Historical Review Press, Richmond (England).

Camus, Albert: 1946, *The Stranger*, Gilbert Stuart (trans.), Vintage, New York.

Carson, Thomas L.: 1981, 'Happiness, Contentment, and the Good Life', *Pacific Philosophical Quarterly* 62, pp. 70–84.

Carson, Thomas L.: 1981, 'The *Übermensch* and Nietzsche's Theory of Value', *International Studies in Philosophy* 13, pp. 9–30.

Coburn, Robert: 1982, 'Morality, Truth, and Relativism', *Ethics* 92, pp. 661–669.

Copleston, Frederick: 1975, *Fredrich Nietzsche: Philosopher of Culture*, Barnes and Noble, New York.

Danto, Arthur: 1965, *Nietzsche as Philosopher*, Macmillan, New York.

Duff, Antony: 1980, 'Desire, Duty, and Moral Absolutes', *Philosophy* 55, pp. 223–238.

Duncker, Karl: 1939, 'Ethical Relativity', *Mind* 48, pp. 39–56.

Edwards, Paul: 1955, *The Logic of Moral Discourse*, Free Press, New York.

Ewing, A. C.: 1970, 'A Suggested Non-Naturalist Analysis of Good', in Hospers and Sellars.

Ewing, A. C.: 1948, *The Definition of Good*, Routledge & Kegan Paul, London.

Falk, W. D.: 1976, 'Hume on Is/Ought', *Canadian Journal of Philosophy* 6, pp. 357–378.

Feldman, Fred.: 1978, *Introductory Ethics*, Prentice-Hall, Englewood Cliffs.

Firth, Roderick: 1954, 'A Reply to Professor Brandt', *Philosophy and Phenomenological Research* 15, pp. 414–421.

Firth, Roderick: 1970, 'Ethical Absolutism and the Ideal Observer', in Hospers and Sellars.

Foot, Philippa: 1978, 'Moral Arguments', in *Virtues and Vices*, University of California Press, Berkeley.

Foot, Philippa: 1967, 'Moral Beliefs', in *Theories of Ethics*, Foot (ed.), Oxford University Press, Oxford.

Frankena, William: 1973, *Ethics*, second ed., Prentice-Hall, Engelwood Cliffs.

Ginzberg, Morris: 1956, *On The Diversity of Morals*, Macmillan, New York.

Gorz, André: 1960, *The Traitor*, Richard Howard (trans.), Calder, London.

Hare, R. M.: 1963, *Freedom and Reason*, The Clarendon Press, Oxford.

Hare, R. M.: 1981, *Moral Thinking*, The Clarendon Press, Oxford.

Hare, R. M.: 1980, 'Nothing Matters', in *The Meaning of Life*, Sanders and Cheney (eds.), Prentice-Hall, Engelwood Cliffs.

Hare, R. M.: 1952, *The Language of Morals*, The Clarendon Press, Oxford.

Harman, Gilbert: 1977, *The Nature of Morality*, Oxford University Press, Oxford.

Harman, Gilbert: 1978, 'What is Moral Relativism?', in *Values and Morals*, A. I. Goldman and J. Kim (eds.), D. Reidel, Dordrecht.

Hartung, Frank: 1954, 'Cultural Relativity and Moral Judgments', *Philosophy of Science* 21, pp. 118–126.

Henson, Richard: 1961, 'Relativism and a Paradox About Meaning', *Philosophical Quarterly* 11, pp. 245–255.

Henson, Richard: 1979, 'What Kant Might Have Said: Moral Worth and the Overdetermination of Dutiful Action', *The Philosophical Review* 88, pp. 39–54.

Herman, Barbara: 1981, 'On the Value of Acting from the Motive of Duty', *The Philosophical Review* 90, pp. 359–382.

Herskovits, Melville J.: 1972, *Cultural Relativism*, Random House, New York.

Herskovits, Melville J.: 1972, *Man and His Works*, Knopf, New York.

Hollingdale, R. J.: 1973, *Nietzsche*, Routledge & Kegan Paul, London.

Hook, Captain: 1954, 'Hook's Tango', from the musical 'Peter Pan', Carolyn Leigh (lyrics), recorded by RCA, New York.

Hospers and Sellars (eds.): 1970, *Readings in Ethical Theory*, second ed., Prentice-Hall, Engelwood Cliffs.

Hume, David: 1888, *A Treatise of Human Nature*, Oxford University Press, Oxford.

Hume, David: 1902, *Enquiry Concerning the Principles of Morals*, Oxford University Press, Oxford.

Husserl, Edmund: 1970, *The Logical Investigations*, J. N. Findlay (trans.), Humanities, New York.

Kant, Immanuel: 1964, *Groundwork of the Metaphysics of Morals*, H. J. Paton (trans.), Harper and Row, New York.

Kaufmann, Walter: 1968, *Nietzsche*, third ed., Princeton University Press, Princeton.

Kierkegaard, Søren: 1963, *Either/Or*, Vol. I, David and Lillian Swenson (trans.), Princeton University Press, Princeton.

Kroeber, A. L.: 1948, *Anthropology*, Harcourt Brace, New York.

Ladd, John (ed.): 1973, *Ethical Relativism*, Wadsworth, Belmont.

Mackie, J. L.: 1978, *Ethics*, Penguin, Middlesex.

Mackie, J. L.: 1946, 'The Refutation of Morals', *Australasian Journal of Philosophy* **26**, pp. 77–90.

McClintock, T. L.: 1963, 'The Argument for Ethical Relativism from the Diversity of Morals', *The Monist* **47**, pp. 528–544.

Mandelbaum, Maurice: 1969, *The Phenomenology of Moral Experience*, Johns Hopkins, Baltimore.

Mercer, C. M.: 1972, *Sympathy and Ethics*, Oxford University Press, Oxford.

Moore, G. E.: 1903, *Principia Ethica*, Cambridge University Press, Cambridge.

Morgan, George: 1941, *What Nietzsche Means*, Harvard University Press, Cambridge.

Munro, D. H.: 1967, *Empiricism and Ethics*, Cambridge University Press, Cambridge.

Nietzsche, Friedrich: 1968, *Anti-Christ* (*AC*), in *Twilight of the Idols and Anti-Christ*, R. J. Hollingdale (trans.), Penguin, Middlesex.

Nietzsche, Friedrich: 1955, *Beyond Good and Evil* (*BG&E*), Marianne Cowan (trans.), Regnery, Chicago.

Nietzsche, Friedrich: 1911, *Dawn of Day* (*DD*), J. M. Kennedy (trans.), Macmillan, New York.

Nietzsche, Friedrich: 1964, *Human All too Human* (*HA*), Helen Zimmern (trans.), Russell and Russell, New York.

Nietzsche, Friedrich: 1967, *On the Genealogy of Morals* (*GM*), in *On the Genealogy of Morals and Ecce Homo* (*EH*), Kaufmann and Hollingdale (trans.), Vintage, New York.

Nietzsche, Friedrich: 1974, *The Gay Science* (*GS*), Walter Kaufmann (trans.), Vintage, New York.

Nietzsche, Friedrich: 1968, *Thus Spoke Zarathustra* (*Z*), in *The Portable Nietzsche*, Walter Kaufmann (trans.), Viking, New York.

Nietzsche, Friedrich: 1968, *The Will to Power* (*WP*), Kaufmann and Hollingdale (trans.), Vintage, New York.

Nietzsche, Friedrich: 1968, *Twilight of the Idols* (*TI*), in *Twilight of the Idols and Anti-Christ*, R. J. Hollingdale (trans.), Penguin, Middlesex.

Nielsen, Kai: 1971, 'Anthropology and Ethics', *Journal of Value Inquiry* **5**, pp. 253–266.

Nielsen, Kai: 1976, 'Ethical Relativism and the Facts of Cultural Relativity', in *Understanding Moral Philosophy*, James Rachels (ed.), Dickenson, Encino.

Olafson, Frederick: 1956, 'Meta-Ethics and the Moral Life', *The Philosophical Review* **65**, pp. 159–178.

Plato: 1961, *Theatetus*, Francis Cornford (trans.), in *The Collected Dialogues of Plato*, Edith Hamilton and Huntington Cairns (eds.), The Bollingen Press, Princeton.

Popper, Karl R.: 1971, *The Open Society and Its Enemies*, fifth ed., Princeton University Press, Princeton.

Postow, B. C.: 1979, 'Dishonest Relativism', *Analysis* **39**, pp. 45–48.

Pritchard, H. A.: 1968, 'Does Moral Philosophy Rest On a Mistake?', in *Moral Obligation*, Oxford University Press, Oxford.

Raphael, D. D.: 1972, 'The Impartial Spectator', *Proceedings of the British Academy* LVIII, pp. 3–22.

Rashdall, Hastings: 1914, *Is Conscience an Emotion?*, T. F. Unwin, London.

Robinson, Richard: 1948, 'The Emotive Theory of Ethics', *Proceedings of the Aristotelian Society*, *Supplementary Volume 22*, pp. 79–106.

Ross, W. D.: 1939, *Foundations of Ethics*, Oxford University Press, Oxford.

Russell, Bertrand: 1944, 'A Reply to My Critics', in *The Philosophy of Bertrand Russell*, P. A. Schilpp (ed.), Tudor, New York.

Sartre, Jean Paul: 1957, *Existentialism and Human Emotions*, B. Frechtman and Hazel Barnes (trans.), Philosophical Library, New York.

Scheler, Max.: 1973, *Ressentiment*, William Holdheim (trans.), Schocken Books, New York.

Scheler, Max.: 1972, *The Nature of Sympathy*, Peter Heath (trans.), Archon Books, Hamden.

Schopenhauer, Arthur: 1965, *On the Basis of Morality*, E. F. J. Payne (trans.), Bobbs-Merrill, Indianapolis.

Shakespeare, William: 1978, *Richard III*, in *The Annotated Shakespeare*, A. L. Rowse (ed.), Orbis, New York.

Sidgwick, Henry: 1966, *The Methods of Ethics*, Dover, New York.

Smith, Adam: 1974, *The Theory of Moral Sentiments*, D. D. Raphael (ed.), The Clarendon Press, Oxford.

Stein, Edith: 1964, *On the Problem of Empathy*, Waltraut Stein (trans.), Martinus Nijhoff, The Hague.

Stevenson, Charles L.: 1944, *Ethics and Language*, Yale, New Haven.

Stevenson, Charles L.: 1970, 'The Emotive Meaning of Ethical Terms', in Hospers and Sellars.

Sumner, W. G.: 1907, *Folkways*, Ginn and Co., New York.

Taurek, John: 1977, 'Should the Numbers Count?', *Philosophy & Public Affairs* **7**, pp. 293–316.

Taylor, Paul: 1961, *Normative Discourse*, Prentice-Hall, Engelwood Cliffs.

Taylor, Paul: 1967, *Problems of Moral Philosophy*, Dickenson, Encino.

Taylor, Paul: 1973, 'Social Science and Ethical Relativism', in Ladd.

Thoreau, Henry David: 1967, 'Civil Disobedience', in *The American Tradition in Literature*, Bradley, Beatty, and Long (eds.), Norton, New York.

Tomas, Vincent: 1950, 'Ethical Disagreement and the Emotive Theory of

Values', *Mind* **60**, pp. 205–222.

Toulmin, Steven: 1970, *Reason in Ethics*, Cambridge University Press, Cambridge.

Urmson, J. O.: 1968, *The Emotive Theory of Ethics*, Oxford University Press, Oxford.

Warnock, G. J.: 1967, *Modern Moral Philosophy*, Macmillan, New York.

Warnock, G. J.: 1971, *The Object of Morality*, Methuen, London.

Wellman, Carl: 1970, 'Emotivism and Ethical Objectivity', in Hospers and Sellars.

Wellman, Carl: 1975, *Morals and Ethics*, Scott Foresman, Glenview.

Westermarck, Edward: 1970, *Ethical Relativity*, Grenwood, Westport.

Wilcox, John: 1974, *Truth and Value in Nietzsche*, University of Michigan Press, Ann Arbor.

Wittgenstein, Ludwig: 1969, *On Certainty*, Anscombe and von Wright (trans.), Blackwell, Oxford.

Wittgenstein, Ludwig: 1953, *Philosophical Investigations*, Anscombe (trans.), Macmillan, New York.

INDEX

PHILOSOPHICAL STUDIES SERIES
IN PHILOSOPHY

Editors:

WILFRID SELLARS, Univ. of Pittsburgh and KEITH LEHRER, Univ. of Arizona

Board of Consulting Editors:

Jonathan Bennett, Allan Gibbard, Robert Stalnaker, and Robert G. Turnbull